MASTER THE™ DSST®

Introduction to World Religions Exam

PETERSON'S®

About Peterson's®

Peterson's has been your trusted educational publisher for over 50 years. It's a milestone we're quite proud of, as we continue to offer the most accurate, dependable, high-quality educational content in the field, providing you with everything you need to succeed. No matter where you are on your academic or professional path, you can rely on Peterson's for its books, online information, expert test-prep tools, the most up-to-date education exploration data, and the highest quality career success resources—everything you need to achieve your education goals. For our complete line of products, visit **www.petersons.com.**

For more information, contact Peterson's, 4380 S. Syracuse St., Suite 200, Denver, CO 80237; 800-338-3282 Ext. 54229; or visit us online at **www.petersons.com**.

© 2020 Peterson's

ISBN-13: 978-0-7689-4460-0

Printed in the United States of America

10 9 8 7 6 5 4 3 2 1   22 21 20

Contents

Before You Begin

HOW THIS BOOK IS ORGANIZED

Peterson's *Master the*™ *DSST® Introduction to World Religions Exam* provides a diagnostic test, subject-matter review, and a post-test.

- **Diagnostic Test**—Twenty multiple-choice questions, followed by an answer key with detailed answer explanations
- **Assessment Grid**—A chart designed to help you identify areas that you need to focus on based on your test results
- **Subject-Matter Review**—General overview of the exam subject, followed by a review of the relevant topics and terminology covered on the exam
- **Post-test**—Sixty multiple-choice questions, followed by an answer key and detailed answer explanations

The purpose of the diagnostic test is to help you figure out what you know—or don't know. The twenty multiple-choice questions are similar to the ones found on the DSST exam, and they should provide you with a good idea of what to expect. Once you take the diagnostic test, check your answers to see how you did. Included with each correct answer is a brief explanation regarding why a specific answer is correct, and in many cases, why other options are incorrect. Use the assessment grid to identify the questions you miss so that you can spend more time reviewing that information later. As with any exam, knowing your weak spots greatly improves your chances of success.

Following the diagnostic test is a subject-matter review. The review summarizes the various topics covered on the DSST exam. Key terms are defined; important concepts are explained; and when appropriate, examples are provided. As you read the review, some of the information may seem familiar while other information may seem foreign. Again, take note of the unfamiliar because that will most likely cause you problems on the actual exam.

After studying the subject-matter review, you should be ready for the post-test. The post-test contains sixty multiple-choice items, and it will serve as a dry run for the real DSST exam. There are complete answer explanations at the end of the test.

OTHER DSST® PRODUCTS BY PETERSON'S

Books, flashcards, practice tests, and videos available online at **www.petersons.com/testprep/dsst**

- A History of the Vietnam War
- Art of the Western World
- Astronomy
- Business Mathematics
- Business Ethics in Society
- Civil War and Reconstruction
- Computing and Information Technology
- Criminal Justice
- Environmental Science
- Ethics In America
- Ethics in Technology
- Foundations in Education
- Fundamentals of Cybersecurity
- General Anthropology
- Health and Human Development
- History of the Soviet Union
- Human Resource Management
- Introduction to Business
- Introduction to Geography
- Introduction to Law Enforcement
- Introduction to World Religions
- Lifespan Developmental Psychology
- Math for Liberal Arts
- Management Information Systems
- Money and Banking
- Organizational Behavior
- Personal Finance
- Introduction to Geology
- Principles of Advanced English Composition
- Principles of Finance
- Principles of Public Speaking
- Principles of Statistics
- Principles of Supervision
- Substance Abuse
- Technical Writing

Like what you see? Get unlimited access to Peterson's full catalog of DSST practice tests, instructional videos, flashcards, and more for **75% off the first month!** Go to **www.petersons.com/testprep/dsst** and use coupon code **DSST2020** at checkout. Offer expires July 1, 2021.

Chapter 1

All About the DSST® Exam

WHAT IS DSST®?

Previously known as the DANTES Subject Standardized Tests, the DSST program provides the opportunity for individuals to earn college credit for what they have learned outside of the traditional classroom. Accepted or administered at more than 1,900 colleges and universities nationwide and approved by the American Council on Education (ACE), the DSST program enables individuals to use the knowledge they have acquired outside the classroom to accomplish their educational and professional goals.

WHY TAKE A DSST® EXAM?

DSST exams offer a way for you to save both time and money in your quest for a college education. Why enroll in a college course in a subject you already understand? For more than 30 years, the DSST program has offered the perfect solution for individuals who are knowledgeable in a specific subject and want to save both time and money. A passing score on a DSST exam provides physical evidence to universities of proficiency in a specific subject. More than 1,900 accredited and respected colleges and universities across the nation award undergraduate credit for passing scores on DSST exams. With the DSST program, individuals can shave months off the time it takes to earn a degree.

The DSST program offers numerous advantages for individuals in all stages of their educational development:

- Adult learners
- College students
- Military personnel

Adult learners desiring college degrees face unique circumstances—demanding work schedules, family responsibilities, and tight budgets. Yet adult learners also have years of valuable work experience that can be applied toward a degree through the DSST program. For example, adult learners with on-the-job experience in business and management might be able to skip the Business 101 courses if they earn passing marks on DSST exams such as Introduction to Business and Principles of Supervision.

Adult learners can put their prior learning into action and move forward with more advanced course work. Adults who have never enrolled in a college course may feel a little uncertain about their abilities. If this describes your situation, then sign up for a DSST exam and see how you do. A passing score may be the boost you need to realize your dream of earning a degree. With family and work commitments, adult learners often feel they lack the time to attend college. The DSST program provides adult learners with the unique opportunity to work toward college degrees without the time constraints of semester-long course work. DSST exams take two hours or less to complete. In one weekend, you could earn credit for multiple college courses.

The DSST exams also benefit students who are already enrolled in a college or university. With college tuition costs on the rise, most students face financial challenges. The fee for each DSST exam starts at $80 (plus administration fees charged by some testing facilities)—significantly less than the $750 average cost of a 3-hour college class. Maximize tuition assistance by taking DSST exams for introductory or mandatory course work. Once you earn a passing score on a DSST exam, you are free to move on to higher-level course work in that subject matter, take desired electives, or focus on courses in a chosen major.

Not only do college students and adult learners profit from DSST exams, but military personnel reap the benefits as well. If you are a member of the armed services at home or abroad, you can initiate your post-military career by taking DSST exams in areas with which you have experience. Military personnel can gain credit anywhere in the world, thanks to the fact that almost all of the tests are available through the internet at designated testing locations. DSST testing facilities are located at more than 500 military installations, so service members on active duty can get a jump-start on a post-military career with the DSST program. As an additional incentive, DANTES (Defense Activity for Non-Traditional Education Support) provides funding for DSST test fees for eligible members of the military.

More than 30 subject-matter tests are available in the fields of Business, Humanities, Math, Physical Science, Social Sciences, and Technology.

Available DSST® Exams

Business	Social Sciences
Business Ethics and Society	A History of the Vietnam War
Business Mathematics	Art of the Western World
Computing and Information Technology	Criminal Justice
Human Resource Management	Foundations of Education
Introduction to Business	Fundamentals of Counseling
Management Information Systems	General Anthropology
Money and Banking	History of the Soviet Union
Organizational Behavior	Introduction to Geography
Personal Finance	Introduction to Law Enforcement
Principles of Finance	Lifespan Developmental Psychology
Principles of Supervision	Substance Abuse
	The Civil War and Reconstruction
Humanities	**Physical Sciences**
Ethics in America	Astronomy
Introduction to World Religions	Environment Science
Principles of Advanced English Composition	Health and Human Development
	Introduction to Geology
Principles of Public Speaking	
Math	**Technology**
Fundamentals of College Algebra	Ethics in Technology
Math for Liberal Arts	Fundamentals of Cybersecurity
Principles of Statistics	Technical Writing

As you can see from the table, the DSST program covers a wide variety of subjects. However, it is important to ask two questions before registering for a DSST exam.

1. Which universities or colleges award credit for passing DSST exams?
2. Which DSST exams are the most relevant to my desired degree and my experience?

Knowing which universities offer DSST credit is important. In all likelihood, a college in your area awards credit for DSST exams, but find out before taking an exam by contacting the university directly. Then review the list of DSST exams to determine which ones are most relevant to the degree you are seeking and to your base of knowledge. Schedule an appointment with your college adviser to determine which exams best fit your degree program and which college courses the DSST exams can replace. Advisers should also be able to tell you the minimum score required on the DSST exam to receive university credit.

DSST® TEST CENTERS

You can find DSST testing locations in community colleges and universities across the country. Check the DSST website (**www.getcollegecredit. com**) for a location near you or contact your local college or university to find out if the school administers DSST exams. Keep in mind that some universities and colleges administer DSST exams only to enrolled students. DSST testing is available to men and women in the armed services at more than 500 military installations around the world.

HOW TO REGISTER FOR A DSST® EXAM

Once you have located a nearby DSST testing facility, you need to contact the testing center to find out the exam administration schedule. Many centers are set up to administer tests via the internet, while others use printed materials. Almost all DSST exams are available as online tests, but the method used depends on the testing center. The cost for each DSST exam starts at $80, and many testing locations charge a fee to cover their costs for administering the tests. Credit cards are the only accepted payment method for taking online DSST exams. Credit card, certified check, and money order are acceptable payment methods for paper-and-pencil tests.

Test takers are allotted two score reports—one mailed to them and another mailed to a designated college or university, if requested. Online tests generate unofficial scores at the end of the test session, while individuals taking paper tests must wait four to six weeks for score reports.

PREPARING FOR A DSST® EXAM

Even though you are knowledgeable in a certain subject matter, you should still prepare for the test to ensure you achieve the highest score possible. The first step in studying for a DSST exam is to find out what will be on the specific test you have chosen. Information regarding test content is located on the DSST fact sheets, which can be downloaded at no cost from **www. getcollegecredit.com**. Each fact sheet outlines the topics covered on a subject-matter test, as well as the approximate percentage assigned to each topic. For example, questions on the World Religions exam are distributed in the following way: Definition and Origins of Religion—5%, Indigenous Religions—5%, Hinduism—11%, Buddhism—11%, Confucianism—6%, Daoism—4%, Shintoism—4%, Judaism—11%, Christianity—18%, Islam—16%, Religious Movements and Syncretism—9%.

In addition to the breakdown of topics on a DSST exam, the fact sheet also lists recommended reference materials. If you do not own the recommended books, then check college bookstores. Avoid paying high prices for new textbooks by looking online for used textbooks. Don't panic if you are unable to locate a specific textbook listed on the fact sheet; the textbooks are merely recommendations. Instead, search for comparable books used in university courses on the specific subject. Current editions are ideal, and it is a good idea to use at least two references when studying for a DSST exam. Of course, the subject matter provided in this book will be a sufficient review for most test takers. However, if you need additional information, then it is a good idea to have some of the reference materials at your disposal when preparing for a DSST exam.

Fact sheets include other useful information in addition to a list of reference materials and topics. Each fact sheet includes subject-specific sample questions like those you will encounter on the DSST exam. The sample questions provide an idea of the types of questions you can expect on the exam. Test questions are multiple-choice with one correct answer and three incorrect choices.

The fact sheet also includes information about the number of credit hours ACE has recommended be awarded by colleges for a passing DSST exam score. However, you should keep in mind that not all universities and colleges adhere to the ACE recommendation for DSST credit hours. Some institutions require DSST exam scores higher than the minimum score recommended by ACE. Once you have acquired appropriate reference materials and you have the outline provided on the fact sheet, you are ready to start studying, which is where this book can help.

TEST DAY

After reviewing the material and taking practice tests, you are finally ready to take your DSST exam. Follow these tips for a successful test day experience.

1. **Arrive on time.** Not only is it courteous to arrive on time to the DSST testing facility, but it also allows plenty of time for you to take care of check-in procedures and settle into your surroundings.
2. **Bring identification.** DSST test facilities require that candidates bring a valid government-issued identification card with a current photo and signature. Acceptable forms of identification include a current driver's license, passport, military identification card, or state-issued identification card. Individuals who fail to bring proper identification to the DSST testing facility will not be allowed to take an exam.
3. **Bring the right supplies.** If your exam requires the use of a calculator, you may bring a calculator that meets the specifications. For paper-based exams, you may also bring No. 2 pencils with an eraser and black ballpoint pens. Regardless of the exam methodology, you are NOT allowed to bring reference or study materials, scratch paper, or electronics such as cell phones, personal handheld devices, cameras, alarm wrist watches, or tape recorders to the testing center.
4. **Take the test.** During the exam, take the time to read each question-and-answer option carefully. Eliminate the choices you know are incorrect to narrow the number of potential answers. If a question completely stumps you, take an educated guess and move on—remember that DSSTs are timed; you will have 2 hours to take the exam.

With the proper preparation, DSST exams will save you both time and money. So join the thousands of people who have already reaped the benefits of DSST exams and move closer than ever to your college degree.

INTRODUCTION TO WORLD RELIGIONS EXAM FACTS

The DSST® Introduction to World Religions exam consists of 100 multiple-choice questions that cover the historical development, doctrine, and practice of religions throughout the world. The exam focuses upon the following topics: dimensions and approaches to religion, primal religions, Hinduism, Buddhism, Confucianism, Daoism, Judaism, Christianity, Islam, Shintoism, and religious movements and syncretism. Careful reading, critical thinking, and logical analysis will be as important as your knowledge of religious doctrines.

Area or Course Equivalent: Introduction to World Religions
Level: Lower-level baccalaureate
Amount of Credit: 3 Semester Hours
Minimum Score: 400
Source: https://www.getcollegecredit.com/wp-content/assets/
factsheets/IntroductionToWorldReligions.pdf

I. Definition and Origins of Religion – 5%

    a. Basic dimensions of religion (e.g. ethics, ritual, doctrine)

    b. Approaches to religion (e.g. natural and revealed theology, descriptive, historical)

II. Indigenous Religions – 5%

    a. Native North American traditions (e.g. Aztec, Inuit, Lakota; Hopi, Cherokee)

    b. Native South American traditions (e.g. Incan, Mapuche)

    c. Native West African traditions (e.g. Yoruba, Dogon, BaVenda)

    d. Native Middle Eastern traditions (e.g. Mesopotamian, Canaanite)

III. Hinduism – 11%

    a. Historical development (e.g. Vedic, Classical, Medieval and Modern periods)

    b. Major traditions (e.g. Theistic paths)

    c. Doctrine and practice (e.g. major philosophical systems, spiritual disciplines [yoga], moksha, festivals)

IV. Buddhism – 11%

    a. Historical development (e.g. life of Buddha)

    b. Major traditions (Theravada, Mahayana and Vajrayana)

    c. Doctrine and practice (e.g. Four Noble Truths, Noble Eight-Fold Path, Three Jewels, rituals, symbols, festivals)

V. Confucianism – 6%

    a. Historical development (e.g. ancient Chinese tradition, life of Confucius, classical Confucianism)

    b. Doctrine and practice (e.g. ritual, filial piety, loyalty, humaneness, genteel behavior, festivals)

VI. Daoism – 4%

    a. Historical development (e.g. ancient Chinese tradition, Lao Tzu)

    b. Doctrine and practice (e.g. Dao, wu wei, rituals)

VII. Shintoism – 4%

    a. Historical development (e.g. influence on Buddhism, influence within Japanese culture, WWII)

    b. Doctrine and practice (e.g. three forms of Shinto, Kami, festivals)

VIII. Judaism – 11%

    a. Historical development (e.g. ancient Israelites, First Temple period, Second Temple period, modern Judaism, The Holocaust, Kabbalah)

    b. Denominations (e.g. Orthodox, Conservative [Masorti], Reform [Liberal/Progressive]; Reconstructionist)

    c. Doctrine and practice (e.g. Torah, Talmud, covenant, rituals, symbols, festivals)

IX. Christianity – 18%

    a. Historical development (e.g. life of Jesus, early church, medieval church, The Reformation, modern church)

    b. Major traditions (e.g. Roman Catholic, Orthodox, Protestant)

    c. Doctrine and practice (e.g. Old and New Testaments, crucifixion and resurrection, Trinity, Creeds, rituals, symbols, liturgical calendar)

X. Islam – 16%

    a. Historical development (e.g., life of Muhammad, rise of Empire, Golden Age, Ottomans/Mughals, modern Islam)

    b. Major traditions (e.g. Sunni, Shi'a, and Sufi)

    c. Doctrine and practice (e.g. Allāh, Qur'an, Five Pillars of Islam, resurrection and judgment; predestination, Sharia/Fiqh; jihad, festivals)

XI. Religious Movements and Syncretism – 9%

    a. Before 1000 C.E. (e.g. Zoroastrianism, Jainism, Mystery Cults)

    b. After 1000 C.E. (e.g. Baha'l, Sikhism)

    c. Contemporary Religious Movements (e.g. Mormonism, Jehovah's Witnesses, Scientology, Nature Spirituality, etc.)

Chapter 2

Introduction to World Religions Diagnostic Test

DIAGNOSTIC TEST ANSWER SHEET

1. Ⓐ Ⓑ Ⓒ Ⓓ
2. Ⓐ Ⓑ Ⓒ Ⓓ
3. Ⓐ Ⓑ Ⓒ Ⓓ
4. Ⓐ Ⓑ Ⓒ Ⓓ
5. Ⓐ Ⓑ Ⓒ Ⓓ
6. Ⓐ Ⓑ Ⓒ Ⓓ
7. Ⓐ Ⓑ Ⓒ Ⓓ

8. Ⓐ Ⓑ Ⓒ Ⓓ
9. Ⓐ Ⓑ Ⓒ Ⓓ
10. Ⓐ Ⓑ Ⓒ Ⓓ
11. Ⓐ Ⓑ Ⓒ Ⓓ
12. Ⓐ Ⓑ Ⓒ Ⓓ
13. Ⓐ Ⓑ Ⓒ Ⓓ
14. Ⓐ Ⓑ Ⓒ Ⓓ

15. Ⓐ Ⓑ Ⓒ Ⓓ
16. Ⓐ Ⓑ Ⓒ Ⓓ
17. Ⓐ Ⓑ Ⓒ Ⓓ
18. Ⓐ Ⓑ Ⓒ Ⓓ
19. Ⓐ Ⓑ Ⓒ Ⓓ
20. Ⓐ Ⓑ Ⓒ Ⓓ

INTRODUCTION TO WORLD RELIGIONS DIAGNOSTIC TEST

24 minutes—20 questions

Directions: Carefully read each of the following 20 questions. Choose the best answer to each question and fill in the corresponding circle on the answer sheet. The Answer Key and Explanations can be found following this Diagnostic Test.

1. Which of the following accurately describes Ramadan?

    A. It is the Muslim month of fasting.
    B. It is the Jewish day of atonement.
    C. It is the forty days before Easter.
    D. It is the Hindu festival of lights.

2. The Hasidim

    A. is a modern denomination of Judaism that follows a liberal interpretation of Jewish law.
    B. are followers of mystical rabbis who live in their own communities separated from the world.
    C. are descended from Jews who were expelled from Spain and Portugal in the fifteenth century.
    D. is a twentieth-century denomination that keeps traditional historical Jewish customs.

3. The purpose of the Second Vatican Council was to

    A. reassert that Confirmation, Penance, the Eucharist, Extreme Unction, Marriage, and Holy Orders, as well as Baptism, were sacraments.
    B. affirm the basic tenets of the faith by developing what became known as the Nicene Creed.
    C. modernize and revitalize the Catholic Church.
    D. reassert Catholic Church teachings after the Protestant Reformation.

4. The basic sacred text of Hinduism is the

   A. *Law of Manu.*
   B. *Vedas.*
   C. *Analects.*
   D. *Bhagavad Gita.*

5. The basic belief system of Zoroastrianism is based on which of the following?

   A. Five Pillars
   B. Four Books
   C. Three-Fold Path
   D. Eight-Fold Path

6. Dimensions of basic religions include

     I. rituals.
     II. taboos.
     III. ancestor worship.
     IV. animism.

   A. I and II only
   B. I and III only
   C. I, II, and IV only
   D. I, II, III, and IV

7. A basic tenet of Confucius' teachings is

   A. the renunciation of all desire in order to enter nirvana.
   B. behaving ethically at all times and in all relationships.
   C. making regular sacrifices to the deities in order to have one's transgressions wiped away.
   D. the balance between dark and light, heaven and earth.

8. In Hinduism, *samsara* is

   A. the force generated by actions in this life that set up what the next life will be like.
   B. the breaking free of life.
   C. the wandering of the life force from one body and time to another.
   D. a riddle that will help a believer achieve insight.

9. The Second Pillar of Islam is

A. daily prayer.
B. almsgiving.
C. hajj.
D. fasting.

10. Daoists believe that human suffering, pain, and violence are eliminated only through a belief in

A. no action, or inaction, which leads individuals to a state of harmony with their own nature.
B. a single, all-powerful God who makes ethical demands and places responsibilities on individuals and community.
C. the practice of ethical relationships that involve reciprocal duties and responsibilities among specific members of society.
D. the idea that the individual, or essential, self is one with Brahman and everything else in the universe.

11. Which of the following is the body of Islamic law?

A. Shi'a
B. Shari'ah
C. Hadith
D. Qur'an

12. A practice common to Protestant denominations in general and the Orthodox Churches is

A. veneration of icons.
B. married clergy.
C. belief in the presence of Jesus in the Eucharist.
D. acceptance of the seven sacraments.

13. Mahavira, who believed that he had found a way to stop the endless cycle of birth, life, and death, is the traditional founder of

A. Ecumenism.
B. Buddhism.
C. Jainism.
D. Daoism.

14. Right views, right thoughts, and right speech are elements of

    A. the right relationships that Confucius taught.
    B. yin and yang.
    C. Jesus' Sermon on the Mount.
    D. Buddhism's Eight-Fold Path.

15. What was the practice of Shinto as a national Japanese religion called?

    A. Shrine Shinto
    B. Folk Shinto
    C. Sect Shinto
    D. State Shinto

16. Which of the following indigenous groups did NOT practice human sacrifice as a part of their worship?

    A. Aztecs
    B. Yoruban
    C. Maya
    D. Inca

17. Passover celebrates the

    A. exodus of the Jews from Egypt.
    B. retaking of the Temple in Jerusalem.
    C. harvest.
    D. delivery of the Jews from Persia.

18. Which of the following men introduced the concept of predestination into Protestantism?

    A. Henry VIII
    B. Martin Luther
    C. John Calvin
    D. John Wesley

19. What is the Buddhist name for the Three Jewels, a symbol that represents the three core values of Buddhism: Buddha, dharma, and sangha?

    A. Triratna.
    B. Dhammapada
    C. Vedas
    D. Dukkha

20. Two important values of the Shinto religion are

    A. poverty and celibacy.
    B. Indra and Agni.
    C. yin and yang.
    D. fertility and family.

ANSWER KEY AND EXPLANATIONS

1. A	**5.** C	**9.** A	**13.** C	**17.** A
2. B	**6.** D	**10.** A	**14.** D	**18.** C
3. C	**7.** B	**11.** B	**15.** D	**19.** A
4. B	**8.** C	**12.** B	**16.** B	**20.** D

1. **The correct answer is A.** During Ramadan, Muslims who are physically able and not pregnant must fast from sunrise to sunset from all food and drink. Choice B describes Yom Kippur, a Jewish holy day. The forty days before Easter (choice C) are known as Lent in the Christian calendar. The Hindu festival of lights (choice D) is called Diwali.

2. **The correct answer is B.** Hasidic Judaism was founded in the eighteenth century in Poland and follows a mystical version of Judaism separated from the modern world. Choice A describes Reform Judaism. Choice C describes Sephardic Jews who might be of any denomination today. Choice D describes Reconstructionist Judaism.

3. **The correct answer is C.** The Second Vatican Council was called by Pope John XXIII in 1962. Its purpose was to modernize and revitalize the Catholic Church. Choice A is incorrect because this reaffirmation was one result of the Council of Trent. Choice D also describes the Council of Trent, not the Second Vatican Council. Choice B is incorrect because the Nicene Creed was promulgated after the First Council of Nicaea in 325.

4. **The correct answer is B.** The *Vedas* is the basic sacred text of Hinduism. The *Law of Manu* (choice A) was written after the *Vedas* and contains ethical and social standards for living, but not all the basic concepts of Hinduism. The *Analects* (choice C) collect the teachings of Confucius. The *Bhagavad Gita* (choice D) is an epic poem about deities and heroes.

5. **The correct answer is C.** To fulfill the will of their god Ahu-ra-Mazda, Zoroastrians follow the three-fold path: good thoughts good words, and good deeds. The Five Pillars (choice A) are the basic belief system of Islam. The *Four Books* (choice B) are part of the basic writings of Confucianism. Choice D is incorrect because Buddhism centers on the Eight-Fold Path.

6. **The correct answer is D.** All four—(I) rituals, (II) taboos, (III) ancestor worship, and (IV) animism—are features of basic religions.

7. **The correct answer is B.** Behaving ethically at all times and in all relationships is a basic tenet of Confucius' teachings. The renunciation of desire to enter nirvana (choice A) is a tenet of Buddhism. Choice C is incorrect because Confucius did not teach about deities, sacrifice to them, or forgiveness of sins. Choice D refers to the concepts of yin and yang in Daoism.

8. **The correct answer is C.** *Samsara* is the wandering of the life force from one body and time to another. Choice A describes karma. Choice B describes moksha. Choice D describes koan, a riddle used in Zen Buddhism to help a person achieve sudden insight.

9. **The correct answer is A.** The first pillar of Islam is "There is no God but Allah; Muhammad is the messenger of Allah." Daily prayer is the second pillar. Almsgiving (choice B) is the third pillar. Fasting (choice D) is the fourth pillar. The hajj, or pilgrimage to Mecca (choice C), is the fifth pillar.

10. **The correct answer is A.** Daoists believe that human suffering, pain, and violence are eliminated only through a belief in no action, or inaction, which leads individuals to a state of harmony with their own nature. Choice B describes the views of Judaism. Choice C describes the practices of Confucianism. Choice D is one of the basic tenets of Hinduism.

11. **The correct answer is B.** Shari'ah is Islamic law. Shi'a (choice A) is one of the two major branches of Islam; the other is Sunni. The Hadith (choice C) is a collection of traditions relating to Muhammad and his companions. Qur'an (choice D) is the basic sacred text of Islam.

12. **The correct answer is B.** Protestant denominations don't have celibacy requirements for priests and ministers, and priests in the Orthodox Churches may be married if they were married before ordination. Choice A is incorrect because icons are not venerated in Protestant denominations. Choice C is incorrect because Protestant denominations do not believe in transubstantiation. Choice D is incorrect because Protestant denominations do not accept all seven sacraments.

13. **The correct answer is C.** Mahavira is the traditional founder of Jainism. Ecumenism (choice A) was a movement by the Roman Catholic, Eastern Orthodox, and some Protestant churches to heal divisions among themselves. Choice B is incorrect because Siddhartha Gautama was the founder of Buddhism. Choice D is incorrect because Lao-zi was the founder of Daoism.

14. **The correct answer is D.** The Eight-Fold Path of Buddhism contains a series of steps: right views, right thoughts, right speech, right action, right livelihood, right effort, right mindfulness, and right concentration. Choice A is incorrect because the teachings of Confucius on right relationships don't specifically use these terms. Choice B is incorrect because yin and yang are elements of Daoism and refer to opposing yet complementary principles of life. Choice C is incorrect because Jesus' Sermon on the Mount includes the Beatitudes.

15. **The correct answer is D.** State Shinto was the national religion of Japan until after World War II. Choice A describes the type of Shinto practiced at outdoor shrines from prehistoric times in Japan. Choice B describes the type of Shinto without any formal doctrine or structure based on Japanese folk beliefs. Choice C describes the Shintoism that is made up of thirteen different sects.

16. **The correct answer is B.** The Yoruban of southeast Nigeria practice a polytheistic religion that centers primarily on Ogun, the god of blacksmiths, warriors, and metal workers and which does not involve human sacrifice. The Aztecs (choice A) believed that human sacrifice could forestall the end of the world. The Maya (choice C) sacrificed humans as a ritual offering of nourishment to their gods. The Inca (choice D) sacrificed children to honor their mountain gods in a ceremonial ritual called capacocha.

17. **The correct answer is A.** Passover celebrates the exodus of the Jews from Egypt. Choice B is incorrect because Chanukah celebrates the retaking of the Temple in Jerusalem. Choice C is incorrect because Sukkoth is a harvest celebration. Choice D is incorrect because Purim celebrates the delivery of the Jews from Persia.

18. **The correct answer is C.** John Calvin introduced the concept of predestination into Protestantism. Choice A is incorrect because, other than substituting his power for that of the Pope, Henry VIII made few changes in the Catholic Church in England. Martin Luther (choice B) did not introduce predestination into Protestantism. John Wesley (choice D) founded Methodism, but he didn't introduce predestination into Protestantism.

19. **The correct answer is A.** Triratna is the Buddhist name for the Three Jewels. Dhammapada (choice B) is the name of a collection of Buddhist proverbs and adages. Vedas (choice C) is the name of the Hindu book of hymns, prayers, and myths. Dukkha (choice D) is the idea that all life is suffering as described in the Four Noble Truths of Buddhism.

20. **The correct answer is D.** Fertility and family are two important values in Shintoism. Poverty and celibacy (choice A) are two important aspects of Theravada Buddhism. Indra and Agni (choice B) are two deities of the Aryans. Yin and yang (choice C) are concepts in Daoism that represent balance.

DIAGNOSTIC TEST ASSESSMENT GRID

Now that you've completed the diagnostic test and read through the answer explanations, you can use your results to target your studying. Find the question numbers from the diagnostic test that you answered incorrectly and highlight or circle them below. Then focus extra attention on the sections dealing with those topics.

Introduction to World Religions		
Content Area	**Topic**	**Question #**
Definition and Origins of Religion	• Basic dimensions of religion • Approaches to religion	6, 13
Indigenous Religions	• Northern Native American traditions • Southern Native American traditions • West African traditions • Ancient Middle Eastern traditions	16
Hinduism	• The history of Hinduism • Major Hindu traditions • Hindu doctrine and practice	4, 8
Buddhism	• The history of Buddhism • Major Buddhist traditions • Buddhist doctrine and practice	14, 19
Confucianism	• The history of Confucianism • Confucian doctrine and practice	7
Daoism	• The history of Daoism • Daoist doctrine and practice	10
Shintoism	• The history of Shintoism • Shinto doctrine and practice	15, 20
Judaism	• The history of Judaism • Denominations • Judaic Doctrine and practice	2, 17
Christianity	• The history of Christianity • Major Christian traditions • Christian doctrine and practice	3, 12, 18

Introduction to World Religions

Content Area	Topic	Question #
Islam	• The history of Islam • Major Islamic traditions • Islamic doctrine and practice	1, 9, 11
Religious Movements and Syncretism	• Before 1000 CE • After 1000 CE • Contemporary religious movements	5

Chapter 3

Introduction to World Religions Subject Review

DEFINITION AND ORIGINS OF RELIGION

Religions—modern and ancient—appear on the surface to be very different, but if you look just a little below the surface, you will find many similarities.

Basic Dimensions of Religion

The Merriam-Webster dictionary defines religion as "the service and worship of God or the supernatural, a commitment or devotion to religious faith or observance, a personalized set or institutionalized system of religious attitudes, beliefs, and practices." Regardless of the religion, all religions, then, have certain characteristics in common: a supernatural aspect, a belief system, and rituals.

In his 1969 work, *The Religious Experience of Mankind,* Ninian Smart describes six characteristics of religion in terms of ritual, mythical, doctrinal, ethical, social, and experiential dimensions:

1. **Ritual:** Rituals are the practices that members of a religion engage in, such as worship (prayer) and fasting. Ritual includes such rites of passage as baptism and confirmation in Christian churches, bar mitzvah and bat mitzvah in Judaism, and marriage in any given religion.
2. **Mythical:** Myths are the stories that provide information about the supernatural aspects of a religion as well as its human actors. "Creation myths" are good examples. These stories may be collected as oral tradition or written down as holy scripture.
3. **Doctrinal:** Doctrine is the belief system that develops within a religion. Doctrine, or dogma, is a body of teachings that defines the truth, values, rituals, and practices of a religion. Some religions have organized and structured written doctrine and others do not.

4. **Ethical:** A religion's doctrine shapes the code of ethics of a religion, that is, the way that members should behave toward themselves and others based on the religion's teachings.

5. **Social:** Religion is social. Religions have members who make up a community and give witness to their faith by their actions.

6. **Experiential:** According to Smart, "personal religion normally involves the hope of, or realization of, experience of that [invisible world of the particular religion]." Being "born again" is an example.

Other writers on the subject of a definition of religion use other categories, such as experience as revelation (showing the invisible world of the supernatural to humans in some way) and faith as response to revelation.

Approaches to Religion

Ancient philosophers and intellectuals have tried since the time of Plato to understand religion and make a rational argument for the existence of God. During the thirteenth century, Thomas Aquinas explored the connections of Christianity to the natural world through the theory of natural theology. Natural theology differed from revealed theology in that it was not based on revelations or knowledge gained from written texts, personal stories, or simple faith. Instead, natural theology attempted to explain God based on the natural world and human reason. Other philosophers later expanded on Aquinas' work. A modern view of natural theology incorporates art, science, history, and morality into a vision where God and religion also fit.

Beginning in the nineteenth century, several different approaches to the study of religion have been popular:

1. **Anthropological:** Anthropologists observe and study the religious elements of a culture, such as its myths, rituals, and taboos. Taboos are those things that adherents of a religion are forbidden to do. For example, Muslims and Jews may not eat pork.

2. **Phenomenological:** Scholars following this school of thought believe that religion is a phenomenon that exists across all cultures and all time. The phenomenological approach has influenced the field of comparative religious studies.

3. **Psychological:** The influence of religion on the thoughts and actions of adherents is the subject of this approach.

4. **Sociological:** This approach considers religion a social rather than a theological phenomenon.

5. **Historical or Descriptive:** This approach applies historical methodologies to collect all of the data and evidence available in order to determine what really happened in past events detailed by a religion. The historical approach determines whether the key figures of a religion really did live at one time or if the events actually took place.

All have their supporters and their critics.

INDIGENOUS RELIGIONS

Indigenous religions have certain features in common, namely: animism (the elements of nature have spirits), magic (control of nature by manipulation), divination (predicting the future), totem (family or clan identification with animals), ancestor veneration or worship, sacrifice, taboo (certain people, places, and things considered either too holy or too "unclean" to touch), myth, ritual, and rites of passage.

Northern Native American Traditions

There is no single Native American religion, but there are certain characteristics that many of these religions share. They are generally animistic and polytheistic. Followers of these religions believe that nature is alive with spirits and that people must live in harmony with nature. Some religions also have a central Supreme Being and a creation story that involves powers or gods creating the world. But, unlike the God of Christianity, Judaism, or Islam, this Supreme Being is above the things of Earth. The spirits of nature, not the Supreme Being, answer the prayers of the people.

Northern Native American religious traditions include ceremonies, rituals, and taboos. Dance and the use of magic are part of many of these practices. There is no special priesthood or hierarchy in northern Native American religions, though some incorporate medicine men and women, sometimes called **shamans**. These individuals have the power to heal, but they also have the power to cause illness and death.

Though it was not typical for northern Native Americans to practice human or animal sacrifice, there is history of human sacrifice and cannibalism occurring in some cultures.

Aztec

The Aztec people lived in central Mexico from the fourteenth to sixteenth centuries and were a warrior culture. According to Aztec legend, the god **Huitzilopochtli**, the god of the sun and war, told the Aztec they would be a great people if they did what he said. They were to go in search of land where they could plant corn and beans. When the time was right, that is, when they were strong enough to defeat any opponent, then and only then should they make war. Any captives they took should be sacrificed to the gods. When the wandering Aztec came to island and saw an eagle sitting on a cactus with a serpent in its beak, the Aztec would know that this was where they should settle.

The Aztec state was a theocracy and a warrior culture, so it is not surprising that Aztec religion was focused on death and the end of the world. Aztecs believed that human sacrifice could forestall the destruction of the world.

Other northern Native American traditions were much less violent than the Aztecs and focused more on pleasing gods through offerings, selfless behavior, and even payment of fines. For example, the **Inuit**, or first peoples of Artic Canada, revere the spirit gods of all things, living and nonliving. Shamans, powerful religious leaders of the Inuit, wear animal masks and instruct people about what prayers and offerings appease the gods, sometimes even assessing fines. They believe that the well-being of their people depends on the pleasure of gods such as Sedna, the goddess of the sea, who only provides food from the ocean if she is pleased with them. Like many Native American cultures, the Inuit have many rules about what they can and cannot do in order to remain in the good graces of the gods.

The Lakota, another Native American culture, are nomadic hunters located in the western plains of the United States. They also practice polytheism and have strong ties to nature and the spirit world. The Lakota religious beliefs hinge on the Sacred White Buffalo Calf Woman, believed to have come to Earth and provided them with the four winds, or directions, to which the Lakota pray. Every prayer is associated with a compass direction, a corresponding color, and a positive or negative connotation. For example, North, or red, is associated with cold, harsh, but cleansing, winds. South, or yellow, represents the origin of the sun, and is the direction to which Lakota pray for wisdom and understanding. Lakota and other tribes also practice **vision quest**, the rite of passage for the young entering puberty. A young man is sent away from his group to live with no food and little else until his vision appears. Often, the vision includes an animal that becomes the young man's totem. People still go on vision quests, usually when faced with a life-defining decision.

The Hopi, a Native American culture of the American southwest desert area, leave their spiritual leadership to the village chiefs. Chiefs lead ceremonies performed in the kivas, or underground adobe buildings, built in each village. The Hopi creation myth involves otherworldly beings who create and destroy worlds based on the behavior of people. The spirits are said to lead men into the world through holes in the grounds of the kivas. Solstice celebrations also feature prominently, as the Hopi try to live in harmony with nature and celebrate all that each season brings.

Probably one of the most famous of the Native American cultures is that of the Cherokee. Located in the American southeast, in the area of Virginia, Tennessee, Georgia, and North and South Carolina, the Cherokee incorporate many elements of nature in their creation stories, traditions, and symbolism. Similar to the Lakota, the four directions of the compass hold special significance for them. The Cherokee believe that the world was created at the new moon, and they worship the sun to ensure good fortune, health, and successful crop yields. Their connection to nature is further solidified in their belief that fire was created by the sun and moon to care for man. Shamans in the Cherokee tradition are identified at birth and often raised separately.

Southern Native American Traditions

Major native cultures of South America were the Mayan, Incan, and Mapuche; each had a distinctive religious tradition.

Mayan

The Mayan culture lived mainly on the Yucatan Peninsula. Predominantly a farming people, their religion centered on deities related to the harvest and included deities associated with rain, soil, sun, moon, and corn. According to the Mayan creation story, all humans were descended from the **Four Fathers** who were created from corn. Maize was the name of the corn god. Human sacrifice was practiced.

Inca

The Inca culture lived in the area that is now Peru, part of Chile, and included northern parts of Argentina. It was a vast expanse ruled by emperors and filled, at its height, with impressive buildings, massive temples, and riches. The Incas' polytheism included numerous gods for nearly every part of nature, including the moon, lake, sea, sun, fire, grain, and so on. Though there are differing versions of the Incan creation story, all integrate nature and aspects of animism. The most popular myth involves two main gods: **Inti** and **Viracocha**. This myth tells how Viracocha rose from the water to revive the world, created people from rocks and clay, gave them language and songs, and created the sun, moon, and stars so that he could see. Inti, the sun god, is said to be the father of the first Incan king. Symbols of the links to nature are apparent in architecture that remains today. Incas believed that **huacas**, or elements of nature that were considered sacred, should be incorporated into niches in buildings so that offerings could be made frequently. Incas also believed that natural elements—caves, mountain peaks, and other objects—all resembled shrines and could be used as places of worship. Inca culture, however, was not without violence. Like the Aztecs, the Inca practiced human and animal sacrifice as a part of their religious tradition.

Mapuche

Another southern Native American culture is that of the indigenous Mapuche people who live in Chile and parts of Argentina. Their culture is a complex one that incorporates polytheism and animism. The Mapuche look to spiritual healers called **machu**, as well as herbalist healers called **ampive**. Their religious beliefs involve Earth's creator, Ñenemapun, a ruler god of Mapuche called Ñenechen, and many gods represented by nature or natural elements, such as the sun, moon, volcanoes, and thunder. The Mapuche hold agriculture and fertility festivals to honor their gods and pray for a good harvest, and their beliefs include an afterlife. In Mapuchen tradition, the forces of evil take the forms of people or of animals, and funeral rites must be performed carefully in order to prevent the **kaku**, or evil witches, from capturing the spirit of the deceased and turning him or her into a ghost.

West African Traditions

Like Native American religions, there is no single African religion, but there are a number of commonalities among them. African religions are typically polytheistic, but have a central **High God** who created the world and withdrew from it. This High God is above all the lesser deities, spirits, and ancestors. The spirits are life forces that inhabit nature.

Animism, ancestor veneration, and divination may be aspects of these religious traditions. Similar to northern Native American traditions, spirits in African religions communicate with humans through dreams and signs, and Africans make offerings and sacrifices to the spirits and ancestors. While these are usually simple—such as an offering of food—animal sacrifices may also be conducted on important occasions. Rites of passage, such as ritual circumcision at puberty, are practiced.

Some traditions, especially in West Africa, have male and female priests and temples, though most do not. They often utilize special curers or healers, similar to medicine men and women. Some African religions also have diviners. In some religions, their powers of foretelling the future are important. In others, diviners are called upon to figure out why people are experiencing various problems.

Yoruban

The Yoruban tradition practiced in southeast Nigeria and Benin offers examples of some commonalities. It includes an all-powerful god called Olorun and a creation story that explains how deities from otherworldly places came to Earth and formed men from clay and rocks. More than 400 lesser gods, or **orisha**, are worshiped by the Yoruban, including one of the most important, **Ogun**, the god of blacksmiths, warriors, and anyone who works with metal. Due to the nature of oral tradition and the need for enslaved Yorubans to hide their religious tradition from their masters, gods' names and genders as well as the details about the tradition's creation story vary slightly from region to region. The Yoruban god **Ifa** represents the tradition's belief that gods can foretell the future. Ifa is believed to use nuts, signs, and squares of the number four to predict the future.

Dogon

The religious traditions of the Dogon people who now live in parts of Mali, in West Africa, are an example of the complexities of an oral tradition that dates back, some believe, as far as Ancient Egypt. The Dogon migrated from their ancestral lands to the areas of Mali and worship ancestors as well as spirits they encountered on their journey. Their creation story involves an amphibian-like creature that may or may not have come from outer space. The Dogon tradition is divided into three important cults: **Awa**, the cult of the dead; **Lebe**, or Earth god; and **Binu**, sacred places and shrines used to honor ancestors and make sacrifices.

Similar to many religions in the African tradition, the Dogon believe in the power of divination. The Dogon look to diviners to interpret patterns they have made in the sand as well as footprints made by foxes, animals considered sacred by the Dogon. These diviners are called upon to answer everyday questions as well as life-changing ones.

Bavenda

Another culture that incorporates animism, ritual, and a belief in a supreme, otherworldly being is the Bavenda, or Venda. Located more centrally in Africa, their supreme being is **Raluvhimba**, a god who created the world and lives in the heavens. The mythical belief system prominently incorporates water at its center. Venda believe that water spirits, or **zwidutwane**, live at the bases of waterfalls and need to be kept happy and fed with offerings of food. These water spirits are half visible in this world and half visible in the spirit world. Venda also revere their ancestors as gods and their king as a living ancestor. Children and elderly are thought to be closest to ancestors, the former because they are so new to this world and the latter because they are so close to leaving this world.

Many of the details of the religious traditions of the Venda are not known to westerners. It is known, however, that Venda incorporate many rituals involving music and dance. Their religious traditions include a coming of age ceremony for young men and women that features a python dance and courtship rituals that involve musical dances with flutes made of bamboo. As with other African religious traditions, the Venda see Raluvhimba and zwidutwane in all aspects of nature, whether it is the rumble of thunder, a flood, or a great harvest. If the gods are not happy, the result is a force of nature.

Ancient Middle Eastern Traditions

The ancient Middle East, or the geographic areas that are now Iran and Egypt, as well as parts of Iraq and Syria, were home to many early religious traditions. Some of the aspects of these early traditions later influenced the major religious traditions of Islam, Christianity, and Judaism that also began in that region of the world and still endure today. Some of these traditions had several important beliefs in common. These included a belief in pleasing god in order to receive benevolent treatment, the belief that god was the source of all existence, mythical stories that explained good and evil, fertility and harvest rituals, and the belief that kings or leaders had some sort of divine lineage. In part due to the difference in climate and geography, the religious traditions of the Mesopotamians, and later the Canaanites, which developed in the area that was Mesopotamia and northern Egypt, varied slightly from the religious traditions that developed in ancient Egypt.

Ancient Egypt

Initially, the sun god **Ra** was the most important Egyptian deity, and all Pharaohs were said to be his sons. He was supplanted by the god **Osiris** who, as god of the afterlife, judged the goodness and evilness of the dead. **Isis**, who was both his wife and sister, was the goddess of magic and familial love. According to the myth, Osiris' brother Set cut Osiris into pieces and scattered him across the earth. Isis brought him back to life. The cult of Isis and Osiris spread across the Middle East and into Greece and the Roman Empire.

In the 1300s BCE, the pharaoh Amenhotep IV introduced worship of a single god, **Aton**. According to Amenhotep, who changed his name to Ikhnaton to honor Aton, Aton was the god of light and truth and had created the world. Ikhnaton became the high priest of the new religion, and worship of Aton became the state religion. After Ikhnaton's death, the worship of Aton ended and Egyptians once again worshiped a variety of deities, including local and regional ones.

Interestingly, the ancient Egyptian religion believed in an afterlife, which was similar to life on Earth and for which pharaohs would need food, clothes, drink, and furniture to make the afterlife as comfortable as this one. They would also need their bodies, which led to the science of mummification. Initially, Egyptians believed that only pharaohs could journey across the river Styx into the afterlife. By the 1500s BCE, however, belief in the afterlife had expanded to include all Egyptians.

Mesopotamians

Like other early religious traditions around the world, the people of what is today known as modern Iran, as well as parts of Iraq, Syria, and Turkey, also had a polytheistic view, and believed that man's goal was to live in harmony with the gods. This area, called Mesopotamia and bordered by the Tigris and Euphrates Rivers, was the birthplace of many civilizations who all shared a belief in the same gods, though oftentimes the names of these gods changed depending on which city-state one lived in.

The people of Mesopotamia believed in a creation story that, like other ancient religions, explained the existence of the cosmos and everything in it. They believed that before man existed, there was only chaotic, swirling water. It was separated into the female principle **Tiamat**, or salt water, and male principle **Apsu**, or fresh water. These gods united; from this union, all other gods were formed.

Apsu was annoyed with the new, younger gods because they were loud and unruly, and so he made plans to kill them. Tiamat heard of these plans and convinced her son Ea, God of Wisdom, to kill Apsu. Ea killed Apsu and created Earth from his body. Angry over Apsu's death, Tiamat conjured the forces of chaos to kill her children, but the great storm god Marduk defeated her and created the sky from her body. He is also said to have created humans as gods' helpers.

Religion played an important part of daily life. Man, it was believed, was created to serve the gods and, in turn, the gods would provide for man through protection, good harvests, and fertility. If man neglected the gods, evil would be inflicted on him. Each town or city-state had a temple that housed a unique patron god, and people believed that the patron god actually resided in the temple. Temple priests were tasked with tending to the patron god, including providing clothing, food, and other human necessities on a daily basis. The temple god was even carried around (in statue form) once a year to visit the city and, on occasion, to visit the temples of other patron gods. In addition to worshiping gods at public temples, individual homes included shrines for personal worship and sacrifice.

Divination was also a large part of the religion of the Mesopotamian cultures. Priests interpreted the will of the gods through the appearances of everyday items, the behavior of birds, dreams, and even the entrails of sacrificial animals. Because the gods had already determined the future, diviners were employed to unravel the messages that described the intent of the gods. Often rulers had personal diviners, while common people had to turn to the services of a local diviner.

Mesopotamians developed intricate legends, stories, and hymns about their gods, some of which later evolved into the stories and hymns of major religions that later developed in this part of the world, such as Zoroastrianism, Judaism, Islam, and Christianity.

Canaanites

Another early civilization of the region, one that developed south of Mesopotamia and north of ancient Egypt, was that of the Canaanites. Like the civilizations of Mesopotamia, they were an agrarian people, and but their religion reflected the importance of fertility and life cycles much more than the religious traditions of Mesopotamia.

The main gods of the Canaanites were **Baalot** and **Baalim**, or **Asherah** when spoken of in the singular. Baalot represented the male gods, or lords, while Baalim represented the female goddesses, or ladies. Both were said to control Earth and the weather. Due to the agrarian nature of the Canaanite civilization, fertility ceremonies, both symbolic and actual, were extremely important. To ensure that the gods would send rain and that harvests would be abundant, temples housed sacred prostitutes. These prostitutes were required to have sexual relations with chosen men who represented Baalot. By impregnating the sacred prostitutes, the community would continue to grow. In addition, the gods would be pleased and send rain and bountiful harvests to the Canaanites.

HINDUISM

There are an estimated one billion Hindus in the world today. The majority live in India and Nepal. They can trace their religion back to the ancient beliefs of the Aryans, a group of nomadic warriors from Central Asia who invaded the Indian subcontinent sometime between 1700 and 1500 BCE.

The History Of Hinduism

The early history of Hinduism is viewed in distinct periods beginning as far back as 2000 BCE. Little is known, however, of the religious practices before the development of the Aryan civilization. The Aryans worshiped deities that represented beauty and the forces of nature. Among them were **Indra**, the female deity of the storm; **Agni**, the female deity of fire; **Varna**, the female deity of the sky; and **Soma**, the male deity of the moon who ruled the stars. The Aryans practiced ritual sacrifices of animals to invoke the deities.

Aryans left records of their religious beliefs and practices in writings that developed into the sacred books of Hinduism. The *Vedas* written during the Vedic period, from 1500 to 500 BCE, are collections of hymns, prayers, myths, rituals, and beliefs about the creation and the deities. The *Vedas* are divided into four collections; the oldest is the *Rigveda* and contains more than a thousand hymns. The *Upanishads* are later writings that were added to the earlier writings and contain advice from Hindu mystics; reincarnation is first mentioned in the *Upanishads*. In all, there are seven books of sacred writings that make up the basic *Vedas*.

During Hinduism's classical period (500 BCE to 500 CE), temple worship grew popular and worship of three of the major sects of Hinduism—Vaishnavism, Shaivism, and Shaktism—developed. More religious writings were produced, resulting in two epic poems of great importance to Hinduism, the *Mahabharata* and the *Ramayana*. The former describes two Indian families who are fighting for control of a kingdom in a bloody war. Within the *Mahabharata* is the poem *Bhagavad Gita*, meaning the "Lord's song." In the poem, the god Krishna and Arjuna, a member of one of the warring families, discuss the meaning of duty. The *Ramayana* tells the story of the wanderings of Prince Rama and his wife Sita who are exiled because of a jealous stepmother.

A later document of importance in the development of Hinduism and written during the classical period is the *Law of Manu*. This ancient text describes **varna**, or the caste system, as already in existence in Hindu society. It is possible that the caste system goes back to the Aryan invaders who considered themselves superior to those they conquered. However the caste system began, it came to divide Hindus into a complex and rigid social system of thousands of different castes, or categories, based on hereditary occupations. The **dalits**, or untouchables, are below the caste system and perform menial manual labor.

The medieval period (500 CE to 1500 CE) saw further development of the Hindu religion, including its assertion over the practices of Buddhism and Jainism as well as the construction of regional temples. The gods Vishnu, Shiva, and Devi (Shakti) rose in popularity during this period of Hinduism.

Hinduism's modern period during the nineteenth and twentieth centuries was marked by its colonization by the British as well as attempts by missionaries to covert Hindus to Christianity. During this same period, Hinduism experienced a renaissance, with spiritual leaders examining their religion closely and undertaking reform efforts. These reformers' views and writings led to the concept of Indian nationalism and the beginning of an effort to export Hinduism to the West.

Major Hindu Traditions

Unlike many religions, Hinduism had no single founder and no single set of revealed dogma. Hinduism has grown and developed internally by incorporating outside influences and is still evolving. It can, however, be organized into four major traditions, or theistic paths, though those paths or sects are loose divisions with much overlap. Many practicing Hindus don't subscribe to any particular theistic path or sect.

Each of the four major theistic paths worships a different god, adheres to a different doctrine about god, and follows a different path to union with god. There are two main doctrines, monoism and inclusive monotheism, and each of the four sects adheres to one of these two beliefs:

- **Monoism:** the belief that there is one impersonal supreme god without qualities or a form and who is represented equally by lesser gods.
- **Inclusive Monotheism:** the belief that there is only one Supreme God who is personal and exhibits qualities and a form, while acknowledging the existence of other, lesser gods.

Each of the four traditions, or sects, is summarized below:

1. **Vaishnavism:** Vaishnavas are personalists and believe in inclusive monotheism, worship Vishnu, and follow the path of devotion, or **bhakti-yoga**.
2. **Shaivism:** Shaivas are impersonalists, or adherents to monoism, who worship Shiva and follow the paths of knowledge (**jnana-yoga**) and meditation (**astanga-yoga**). Asceticism, or self-denial to achieve a spiritual state, is very common among Shaivas.
3. **Shaktism:** This sect is less developed than others and is based on Shaivism. Shaktas are impersonalists, or adherents to monoism, and are most aligned with **karma-yoga**, the path of action. They worship Shakti, or Devi, the female goddess said to be a force of cosmic energy.
4. **Smartism:** Smartas are also monists, believing that god is impersonal. They worship all five deities, whom they treat with the same reverence: Vishnu, Shiva, Shakti (Devi), Ganesh, and Surya. They are impersonalists who adhere to the path of **jnana-yoga**, the path of knowledge. Smartas are liberal and nonsectarian, accepting of all Hindu gods.

Hindu Doctrine and Practice

Hinduism has both a central creator of the world known as **Brahma** and many other deities. Some are avatars of Brahma. The three major deities, or triad, of Hinduism, are Brahma; Vishnu, the preserver; and Shiva, both destroyer and regenerator. Other important deities are Krishna and Rama, both incarnations of Vishnu, and Shakti, also known as Parvati and Kali, among other names, and the wife of Shiva.

TIP: Brahman is the Ultimate Reality, Brahma is the creator, and a Brahmin is a member of the priestly caste.

Basic Hindu beliefs involve the following:

- **Nature of Reality:** All reality is one with Brahman, the Ultimate Reality. The individual, or essential, self is called **atman** and is one with Brahman and everything else in the universe. Everything is simply a representation of Brahman, the formless, nameless, changeless reality.
- **Samsara:** Hindus believe that life is a cycle of birth, life, and death, which they call samsara.
- **Karma:** In what form a person is reborn depends on the law of karma: the actions that an individual performs while living determines future lives. Each reincarnation is the result of previous lives. Do good now and it will be reflected in future lives; do evil and that, too, will be reflected. Good actions raise the status of future lives and evil actions lower future castes.
- **Moksha:** Moksha is release from samsara, which comes with enlightenment. The purpose of the cycle of reincarnations is spiritual progress to reach moksha. Individuals can choose the path of renunciation and find enlightenment or choose the path of desire and continue the cycle of birth, life, and death.
- **Dharma:** Dharma is the rules and duties for Hindus that provide a guide for living. The goal is to act with detachment; that is, people need to destroy desire if they are to achieve moksha.
- **Stages of Life:** Hinduism sets four stages to progress to enlightenment: *student*; *householder*; *anchorite*, a person living in seclusion to meditate and study; and *sannyasi*, a holy man wandering among the people.
- **Ahimsa:** This is the concept of "do no harm," or acting always in a nonviolent manner.

Yoga

The goal of yoga is to free the mind of distractions, so atman can become more open to the Ultimate. There are several schools of yoga, including karma, raja, bhakti, jnana, hatha, and kundalini.

Holy Days

Certain holy days are more prevalent in some areas of India than in others. Major Hindu holy days include:

- **Diwali:** Festival of lights that occurs in autumn and includes a thorough housecleaning to welcome Laksmi, the female deity of wealth
- **Durga Puja:** Celebrates the female deity Durga and the triumph of good over evil; occurs in autumn
- **Krishna Janmashtami:** Celebrates the birth of Krishna and includes fasting for 24 hours; occurs in late summer
- **Ram Navmi:** Celebrates the birth of Rama, an incarnation of Vishnu; occurs in spring

BUDDHISM

Buddhism began as an offshoot of Hinduism. Like Christianity and Islam, Buddhism has a single, historical founder, **Siddhartha Gautama**.

The History of Buddhism

Buddhism was founded by Siddhartha Gautama who lived in the 500s BCE. The son of a wealthy and powerful family, his life changed at the age of 29. Leaving his palace one day, he met an old man, a sick man, a corpse, and a beggar. The misery, sorrow, and decay of life made a great impression on him. In what is known as the **Great Renunciation**, Gautama gave up his riches and left his family to search for an answer to samsara, the Hindu cycle of birth, life, and death. He studied with a variety of teachers but found their teachings unsatisfying. He tried penance and self-mortification, but they, too, seemed lacking to him.

Finally, one night while practicing yoga and meditation, enlightenment came to him. He realized that the answer was choosing a life that took the middle path between asceticism and indulgence, or desire. That night, Gautama became the Buddha, the fully enlightened one. Gautama Buddha, as he was known from then on, spent the next forty-five years of his life on Earth teaching the middle path.

Buddhism expanded across India over the next 200 years. Monasticism as a way of life developed as some disciples built monasteries and became monks and nuns devoted to prayer and meditation. By the third century BCE, the teachings (or dharma) of Buddhism were spreading outside India to what are today Sri Lanka, Myanmar, and Nepal; the nations of Southeast Asia, and eventually to Korea and Japan.

Major Buddhist Traditions

Buddhism has evolved into several thousand sects. Theravada and Mahayana are the principle sects; Theravada is the more conservative. Vajrayana Buddhism is another form of Buddhism practiced mostly in the country of Tibet. Authorities on the subject disagree whether Vajrayana is a third, distinct sect or a variation that came out of the Mahayanan tradition. Unlike Hinduism, Buddhism does not have multiple deities, nor is there a supreme ultimate being.

- **Theravada Buddhism:** This is the path of poverty and celibacy embraced by those men who choose to live as monks. They believe that individuals must achieve enlightenment on their own through meditation and actions, as Gautama Buddha did. When a man achieves enlightenment, he becomes an arhat and is released from samsara at death. However, not all Theravada Buddhists choose monasticism as a way of life. Some men make only a limited commitment to the monastic life. Women may not become monks; however, they can support them with offerings. In this way, they can make merit, that is, influence their karmaic destiny. Theravada Buddhism is practiced today mainly in Thailand, Cambodia, Vietnam, Laos, Myanmar, and Sri Lanka.
- **Mahayana Buddhism:** Most Buddhists belong to this sect. Gautama Buddha's compassion is a central focus. Mahayana Buddhists believe that Gautama Buddha was close to godlike and visited Earth to aid humans. They also believe that he was only one among many Buddhas who are on Earth to help humans. The ideal became bodhisattvas, or Buddhas-in-waiting who, though worthy of nirvana, remain on Earth to help others achieve enlightenment. Unlike Theravada Buddhists who rely on their own efforts, Mahayana Buddhists believe that devotion to Buddhas and bodhisattvas can aid in their efforts to achieve nirvana. Mahayana Buddhism is practiced mainly in China, Tibet, Nepal, Korea, and Japan. Two important forms of Mahayana Buddhism are the following:
  1. **Zen Buddhism:** This sect of Mahayana Buddhism became popular among some Japanese after its introduction from China around 400 CE. Adherents of Zen believe that the Buddha-nature is all around, and only through meditation will humans be able to discover and understand it and, thus, reach enlightenment. Zen Buddhists use riddles called **koans** to aid them in finding enlightenment.

2. **Vajrayana Buddhism (also known as Tibetan Buddhism or Lamaism):** Mahayana Buddhism was originally brought to Tibet in the 600s CE, but over the centuries, it has evolved in unique ways. While many of the practices of Vajrayana Buddhism are similar to those of other forms of Buddhism, it relies heavily on magic; has a priestly class known as lamas; recites the phrase "Om, the jewel of the lotus, hum" to address the Bodhisattva Avalokiteshvara, the patron of Tibet; and uses a prayer wheel to "say" prayers. The chief lama among lamas is the Dalai Lama, who is not only the spiritual leader of Tibetans but also considered the temporal ruler.

Buddist Doctrine and Practice

Buddhism centers on the **Four Noble Truths** and the **Eight-Fold Path**. The Four Noble Truths are as follows:

1. All life is suffering, called **dukkha**.
2. The source of all suffering is desire, attachment to self.
3. The cessation of desire is the way to end suffering.
4. The path to the cessation of desire is the Eight-Fold Path.

The Eight-Fold Path is right understanding, right thought, right speech, right action, right livelihood, right effort, right mindfulness, and right concentration. People are doomed to samsara because of desire. If people can eliminate desire, they will achieve **nirvana**, the release from their karma and, thus, from samsara.

Another important concept in Buddhism is compassion for all living things, which is exemplified by Gautama Buddha's life. Like Hindus, Buddhists practice **ahimsa**, or nonviolence to all things. While monasticism became important, Buddhism did not reject those who chose to live in the world. It welcomed anyone who was trying to live up to the standards of Buddhist teachings and was also willing to support Buddhist monks and nuns.

Rituals

All schools of Buddhism incorporate similar rituals. Meditation is the most common form of Buddhist ritual, helping practitioners find enlightenment. In Tibetan Buddhism, mantras, or sacred sounds that help the practitioner focus and commune with deities, are frequently used. Mudras, or symbolic hand gestures, are less common but still used as Buddhist ritual to aid in meditation. Finally, pilgrimages to Buddha's birthplace, the site of his first teaching, the place he received enlightenment, and the site where he achieved Parinirvana are the most sacred rituals in all of Buddhism.

Three Jewels of Buddhism

Imagery from ancient texts shows the symbol of three jewels, or the **Triratna**, often found in the depiction of Buddha's footprint. This symbol is a metaphor for the three most important aspects of Buddhism: Buddha himself; the dharma, or Buddha's teachings; and the **sangha**, or community of followers. Each of these three aspects of Buddhism is represented by a different colored jewel. Followers, practitioners as well as those taking steps toward ordination, are said to take refuge in these three jewels. Taking refuge can mean following the path to enlightenment, as well as turning to Buddha, his teachings, or the community as a way of dealing with the trials of everyday life.

Sacred Writings

The two main branches of Buddhism have their own sacred writings. The major works of Theravada Buddhism are the Tripitaka (rules and regulations for Buddhist monasteries, life and teachings of Gautama Buddha, and dictionary and teachings) and Dhammapada (collection of proverbs and adages). Among the major works of Mahayana Buddhism are the Lotus Sutra, Heart Sutras, Tibetan Book of the Dead, and Translation of the Word of the Buddha. *Sutra* in Buddhism means "a collection of the stories and teachings of Gautama Buddha." (In Hindu, *sutra* means "a collection of sayings about Vedic doctrine.")

Holy Days

The various sects have their own holy days and celebrations, but common ones are Buddha Day, April 8, honoring the birth of Buddha; Nirvana Day, February 15, observing his death; and Bodhi Day, December 8, celebrating the day he sat down under the Bodhi tree to achieve enlightenment. Days of the month when the moon is full or new are also of great importance to Buddhists.

There are also a number of rites of passage in Buddhism, including marriage, pregnancy, birth, adolescence, and, ultimately, death.

CONFUCIANISM

Confucianism is a philosophy—an ethical code of living—rather than a religion. There is no central supreme being who created the world. However, there is a respect for the past, including ancestors; a focus on humane treatment of one another; and a belief in the duty of the government to provide for the well-being of the governed.

The History of Confucianism

Confucianism takes its name from **Confucius**, who lived from 551 BCE to 479 BCE. Around that time, China was undergoing what has come to be called the Warring States Period. A group of independent states was vying for control of China. This lasted until the third century BCE when the Han dynasty consolidated its power and ruled China for 400 years. Over the centuries, Confucian principles came to dominate Chinese government regardless of the dynasty in power; Confucian teachings and their evolution by government bureaucrats provided an orderly structure for society and governance.

An especially important concept in this development was the Confucian idea of the state as family; family was the basic element of society in Confucian teaching. The emperor was the father of all Chinese and responsible to an impersonal force known as Heaven for the well-being of his people/children. If he did not live up to his role, the people had a mandate from Heaven to replace him. In this way, dynasties rose and fell in China for centuries. Claiming that the current emperor was not working in the best interests of the people, a rival would depose him, calling on the mandate of Heaven as his authority. In this way, Confucianism was used by various rulers over the centuries to cement their position as supreme earthly rulers.

Another aspect of Confucianism that shaped Chinese society was its influence on the Chinese educational system. In order to advance in the Chinese bureaucracy, a position of prestige and power, a man needed to be educated. Confucianist principles became the focus of this education and centered on learning what constituted right action. The reliance on Confucianism resulted in the development of a conservatism in Chinese society that lasted until the Communist Party came to power in the twentieth century.

Confucian Doctrine and Practice

Confucius taught that five relationships exist that involve reciprocal duties and responsibilities, or right action, between:

1. Ruler and subject
2. Father and son
3. Elder brother and younger brother
4. Husband and wife
5. Friend and friend

With the exception of the last relationship, each relationship involves a superior and a subordinate, that is, one person is subject to the other. The subordinate owes loving obedience to the superior, and the superior has a loving responsibility to see to the well-being of the subordinate. Friends owe each other the same responsibility. The correct behavior, or conduct, between the individuals in these relationships is known as **li**.

In addition to these ethical relationships, Confucius taught the concept of **jen**, or humaneness, also described as sympathy, benevolence, or love toward others. Unlike many Eastern religions, Confucius did not see the proper role of humans as self-absorbed in meditation and isolated from one another. He felt that people needed to work toward becoming **junzi**, or genteel, superior, humane beings.

Through education and adherence to moral ways, and with much practice, Confucius believed that people could achieve junzi. His goal was to create harmony in society. Other key concepts include **zhong**, or loyalty to one's true nature, and **xiao**, or filial piety.

Filial piety, or respect for one's parents, was part of Chinese culture prior to Confucius' teachings. Families showed respect for their ancestors and family elders, and in that respect filial piety existed. Confucius expanded on the concept. He felt that it was impossible to repay one's parents for the care and love they have provided their children, particularly during the early years when children are helpless. He felt it was impossible to be a virtuous individual without showing filial piety while parents were alive and even after they were dead. Confucius believed that children should take care of their parents, bury them properly when the time came, provide them with a male heir, and never speak ill of them, even years after they had passed on.

Important Works

The **Five Classics** and the **Four Books** make up the basic writings of Confucianism. Three books to remember are the *Analects of Confucius*, one of the Four Books; *Yi jing*, the first of the Five Classics; and *Book of Mencius* (Meng-Zi). The *Analects* are stories and sayings of Confucius that his followers collected, the *Yi jing* is a book of divination, and the *Book of Mencius* is a defense of Confucian teachings by Mencius, a later Confucian scholar. Mencius took the position that human nature is good. Hsun Tzu (Xun-Zi), an even later Confucian scholar, took the opposite position, that human nature is evil.

DAOISM

Daoism developed slightly later in China than Confucianism and is based on a belief in the naturalness of all things. Its spirituality is a complement to the structure and rigid etiquette required in Confucianism rather than a rival belief system.

The History of Daosim

The beginnings of Daoism date to the 400s and 300s BCE. The traditional founder is considered to be **Lao-zi**, who is also credited with writing the *Dao de jing*, the basis of Daoism. The word *Dao* means "the way." It is possible, however, that the *Dao de jing* is actually a collection of writings of earlier ancient scholars. A second important work is the slightly later *Zhuang-zi* by a man of the same name; it is a collection of parables and allegories.

Initially, Daoism was a philosophy, but it took on religious elements over the centuries. The majority of Chinese people were farmers who saw a relationship between nature as described in Daoism and the deities who were part of their daily lives. Daoism was also influenced by Mahayana Buddhism and adapted some of its rituals and the concept of priesthood. Daoism, in turn, influenced Zen Buddhism's focus on nature.

Daoist Doctrine and Practice

What is the Dao? According to Daoists, the Dao cannot be defined. It is without measure, shape, or characteristics; it is infinite and unceasing. It simply flows "without motive and without effort." The Dao gives life to all things, but, more than life, it gives all things their natures. The Dao is why a human is a human and not a dog or a horse.

The central focus of Daoism is **naturalness**. Human suffering, pain, and violence are the result of the opposite of naturalness—unnaturalness. At one time, people lived a natural life, unhampered by the conventions and restrictions of society. They had been "in harmony with their nature and with the Dao." This harmony began to change with the introduction by society of social conventions and notions of right and wrong as well as people's growing desire for things outside themselves—whether the possession of material goods or of knowledge. Knowledge is a problem because it leads to ideas that interfere with the spontaneity of oneness with the Dao.

To free themselves, Daoists believe that people must become one with the Dao, and then they will realize that all is one with the Dao. There is no reason or need to seek possessions or knowledge. Instead of right action, Daoists believe in no action, or inaction, a concept called **wu wei**. Daoists also apply this idea to government. In essence, the government that governs the least, governs best. A ruler who follows the Dao will govern without seeming to govern, ensuring that the people are fed, living in peace, and free of worry.

A basic teaching of Daoism is the concept of **yin and yang**. The symbol for yin and yang is a circle with two interlocking black and white sections. The white section has a smaller black circle within it, and the black section has a smaller white circle within it. The black represents yin—earth, female, dark, and passive—whereas the white is the yang, the active principle that represents heaven, male, and light. These two basic forces, or things, are not static, as depicted by their symbols, and depend on each other. They must work together in harmony in order to exist.

Meditation is an important vehicle for achieving oneness with the Dao. Unlike Zen Buddhism, which focuses on physical cleansing, Daoism asks adherents to purge their minds of thoughts, thus opening themselves to the Dao. Dao rituals incorporate meditation, along with purification and offerings to deities. Some, such as **jiao**, the ritual of cosmic renewal, are so complex that only Dao priests and their assistants can perform the required chants, music, and prayers. A shorter, less complex jiao ritual still manages to involve every household in a village and has several smaller rituals within it. Temple prayers and chants are also part of the practice of Daoism to honor gods and regulate the balance of yin and yang.

SHINTOISM

The indigenous faith of the Japanese people, Shintoism has no specific founder, religious texts, or gods in the traditional Western sense. It is as old as Japan, and its origin stories explain the existence of Japan and its superiority above all other nations and their peoples. In Shinto teachings, the divine resides in all things in nature from rocks to rainfall, as well as in important ideas or concepts. The word *Shinto* means "the way of the kami," and **kami** are the spirits, or essences, of the natural world. The geography and climate of Japan influenced how the Japanese view the connection among its people, nature, and the divine.

The History of Shintoism

The *Kojiko*, or *Records of Ancient Matters*, written in 712 CE, explains the origins of Shintoism. It is a record of the oral traditions handed down over centuries. Shintoists believe that in the chaos of the beginnings of the universe, when heaven and earth were formed, gods emerged and gave birth to two kami, a brother and sister named Izanagi and Izanami, respectively. These two kami used a jeweled spear to stir the ocean, and thus the first landform—the main island of Japan—was formed. Izanagi and Izanami united and formed the remaining islands of Japan as well as many other kami. This mythological beginning substantiates the belief that Japan and its people are chosen above all others.

Shintoism has many kami, some of them everyday objects and others concepts or ideas. The more important kami include:

- **Amaterasu**, the Sun Goddess, believed to be an ancestor of the Imperial family
- **Benten** or **Benzaiten**, a female kami of music and art with Indian origins
- **Ebisu**, a kami who brings prosperity
- **Susanoo**, the kami of wind who can cause, or protect people from, disasters
- **Tenjen**, the kami of education who grants people success in their exams

Buddhism was introduced to Japan in the sixth century CE, and Shintoism and Buddhism began a struggle that would last centuries. Buddhist, and later Confucian, elements and teachings were introduced to Shintoism. Shinto shrines were turned into Buddhist temples, and some were overseen by Buddhist priests. During this period, the idea that rulers should follow the will of the gods when governing become very popular in Japan. Buddhist, Confucian, and Shinto practices were followed by all in order to ensure the kami protected Japan and its people.

During later centuries, the practice of Shintoism continued to be influenced by Buddhism and then later by Christian missionaries. Eventually, during the Mejii period, Shintoism was separated from Buddhism and became the official religion of Japan. This period of Shintoism is referred to as **State Shintoism**. Though Shinto and Buddhist elements were again separated and temples turned back into Shinto shrines, this separation didn't last. Eventually, Shintoism and Buddhism learned to coexist. Buddhists came to view the kami of Shintoism as manifestations of Buddha. State Shinto fostered nationalism and patriotism among the Japanese, making Shinto priests government officials and supporting tens of thousands of shrines with state funds. However, at the request of Allied Forces following World War II, Japan disbanded its national religion and permanently separated religion and government.

Shintoism can be broken into three categories: Shrine Shinto, Sect Shinto, and Folk Shinto. **Shrine Shinto** is the form of Shinto closest to what was practiced during prehistoric times in Japan and includes State Shinto in its history. Those who practice Shrine Shinto today worship at outdoor public shrines that were funded by the Japanese government during the days of State Shintoism.

Sect Shinto is another form of Shintoism that began in the nineteenth century and is differentiated from other versions of Shintoism by the thirteen different sects that are officially recognized by the Japanese government.

Folk Shinto is Japanese folk belief, without any formal doctrine or organizational structure. It is practiced by rural Japanese at small shrines in the countryside.

Shinto Doctrine and Practice

Men and women can be Shinto priests and can marry and have children. Priests live on the grounds of the shrines, caring for them and overseeing worship and festivals. Shinto shrines integrate natural surroundings to show respect to the kami, and Shintoists make offerings in an attempt to keep evil away and to remain in the good graces of the kami.

Festivals and Rituals

Shinto practitioners hold festivals and rituals to honor ancestors, pray for bountiful harvests, give thanks, and ward off evil spirits. These include music and dance, as well as offerings of all types of food that participants share in. Shinto festivals reflect the influence of the farming culture in Japan and are held at turning points during the seasons; spring festivals ask deities for a bountiful harvest, while autumn festivals thank deities for a bountiful harvest. The Grand Purification Ritual, performed on December 31, cleanses Shinto practitioners of all sin, impurities, and misfortune. By doing so on the last day of the year, they begin the new year unencumbered.

In addition to worshiping at outdoor public shrines, many Shinto practitioners build shrines in their homes, where, it is believed, their ancestors reside. Having a shrine in the home allows practitioners to make daily offerings to ancestors. Two of the important values of Shinto are fertility and family, including ancestor veneration and social cooperation. Worship of ancestors and the deities in nature is called **matsuri**. Prior to entering shrines, Shintoists perform purification rituals, including washing their hands and rinsing their mouths to cleanse themselves of dirt.

The most revered Shinto shrine in Japan is called the Ise Jingu (Grand Shrine of Ise). Amaterasu-Omikami, the sun goddess, has been worshiped at the Ise Jingu for 2,000 years. Toyouke-Omikami, the guardian of well-being, is also worshiped at Ise Jingu. Here Shintoists make offerings to honor the sun goddess and in hopes of receiving protection for clothing, shelter, and food. More than 1,500 ceremonies are performed at this shrine each year. Every twenty years, the buildings at this shrine are dismantled and put back together, piece by piece. The artifacts are refurbished, and the deities receive new clothing. This process ensures that traditions are passed on to younger generations, while refreshing the minds and faith of Shinto practitioners.

JUDAISM

The Hebrews, or Israelites, were unique in the history of world religions up to that point in time in basing their national identity on a "single, all-powerful God who made ethical demands and placed responsibilities on them as individuals and as a community," according to the authors of *The Heritage of World Civilizations*.

The History of Judaism

The Hebrews, under the leadership of Abraham, probably arrived in the area of Mesopotamia sometime between 1900 and 1600 BCE. Some stayed in what was to become known as Palestine, but others moved to Egypt, where they were enslaved. Moses led the Hebrews out of Egypt around the beginning of the thirteenth century BCE, and they settled in Canaan, a region of Palestine, which the Bible calls their Promised Land. The Hebrews built a successful kingdom for some 300 years under rulers such as David and Solomon during what is considered to be the First Temple Period. During this period, Solomon built the Temple to God. In the 800s BCE, the kingdom split into the kingdoms of Judah, formed by ten tribes, and Israel, formed by two tribes.

Over the next centuries, foreign peoples invaded and conquered the two kingdoms. The northern kingdom of Israel disappeared entirely. The southern kingdom, which included the Temple in Jerusalem, was conquered by the Babylonians in the mid-500s BCE. The temple was destroyed and the people taken to Babylon in what is called the **Babylonian Captivity**. They returned to Judah after the defeat of the Babylonians in 539 BCE and rebuilt the Temple more than twenty years after their return from the Babylonian Captivity. This period is referred to the Second Temple Period, and it ended when the Romans, their new captors, destroyed the second temple in 70 CE and again in 132 CE.

The first mention of the Covenant between the Hebrews and the god Yahweh is in the Hebrew Bible's account of Abraham. The reaffirmation of the Covenant came on Mount Sinai, when Moses received the **Ten Commandments**. In exchange for obeying these laws, the Jews would receive Yahweh's protection. Troubles such as foreign conquests were the result of the Jews' failure to abide by their part of the Covenant. Prophets such as Jeremiah and Ezekiel were sent to remind the Jews of their Covenant and of the one true God, Yahweh.

Throughout these periods of subjugation, the Jews retained their religion and their sense of being God's chosen people. The Diaspora, or dispersion of the Jews, began after Assyrians conquered the Kingdom of Israel in 721 BCE, and led to the development of the synagogue as a local center of worship, the position of rabbi as teacher, kosher food laws, and the Sabbath as day of worship.

The Diaspora continued after the Jewish revolt of 66 CE, when the Romans conquered the area, renamed it, and forbade the Jews to enter Jerusalem. Many Jews moved into Western Europe. Over time, they became known as the Sephardim and settled in Spain. Persecuted there during the Inquisition, they fled to Portugal, the Netherlands, North Africa, the Balkans, and the Americas. German Jews became known as Ashkenazi. After persecution there, they moved into Eastern Europe. Ashkenazi and Sephardic Jews have different languages, rituals, and traditions. In the early 1900s, more than a half million Jews lived in Germany. The rise of anti-Semitism and the growing power of the Nazi party led to a systemic and methodical curtailing of the rights of German Jews. Many German Jews fled; those who did not were denied the right to work, subject to quota systems, gathered up and sent to ghettos, and eventually killed in the genocide known today as the Holocaust. By the end of World War II, 6 million Jews had been murdered by the Nazi regime.

Denominations

Modern Judaism has four main divisions, or movements: **Orthodox**, **Conservative**, **Reform**, and **Reconstruction**. The differences revolve around how strictly each interprets the laws and traditions of Judaism, including the place of women. Although the term may be confusing, Conservative Jews are less conservative than Orthodox Jews. The latter, for example, do not allow women to become rabbis and cantors, whereas Conservative, Reform, and Reconstructionist Jews do. Orthodox Jews also require that the sexes be separated in synagogues. While Orthodox Jews eat kosher at home and outside the home, Conservative Jews typically keep kosher at home but may eat nonkosher outside the home, and Reform Jews typically do not observe kosher rules. Reconstructionist Jews and Reform Jews have many practices in common, although Reconstructionist Jews tend to follow more of the traditional historical practices of Judaism. Mordecai M. Kaplan is considered the founder of Reconstructionism in the 1930s.

Orthodox Judaism is the largest group within Judaism and is further divided into Modern Orthodox and Hasidic. Hasidic Judaism was founded in the mid-1700s in Poland by Israel ben Eliezer, who came to be known as Baal Shem Tov. He taught a simple faith that included elements of mysticism; he wanted Jews to maintain their identity and traditions and live within their own enclaves separated from non-Jews. Hasidic Judaism attracted many followers in Eastern Europe. The spiritual leader of a group of Hasidic Jews is known as a **rebbe**, and a rebbe is descended from a line of rebbes. Another important leader of Judaism was the nineteenth-century German philosopher and writer Moses Mendelssohn. He encouraged Jews to leave their ghettoes and live within the larger society.

Judaic Doctrine and Practice

The Hebrews, who were surrounded by neighbors worshiping many gods, were unique in adopting monotheism, the worship of one God. The basic teachings of Judaism are Yahweh (God) is the supreme creator, Yahweh will send a messiah to redeem the world, and the Jews are God's chosen people. Yahweh formed a covenant with the Jews, who, in return for offering obedience to the Law and worshiping only Yahweh, would become a great nation. The sense of Judaism as a community of believers is of central importance.

The Ten Commandments are the ethical code of Judaism—the Law—given by Yahweh to the Hebrews as a guide to moral living. A slightly shortened version of the Decalogue is the following:

1. I am the Lord thy God.
2. Thou shall have no other gods before Me.
3. Thou shall not take the name of the Lord thy God in vain.
4. Remember the Sabbath Day.
5. Honor thy father and thy mother.
6. Thou shall not kill.
7. Thou shall not commit adultery.
8. Thou shall not steal.
9. Thou shall not bear false witness against thy neighbor.
10. Thou shall not covet thy neighbor's goods.

Moses received these commandments on Mount Sinai during the forty years that the Hebrews wandered in the desert after their exodus from Egypt.

Writings

The Jewish sacred writings are the Hebrew Bible and Talmud. The Bible contains the Pentateuch, Prophets, and the Ketuvim. The Pentateuch is also known as the Torah or the Five Books of Moses; these are the first five books of the Bible. The Prophets contain the writing of the major prophets (Jeremiah, Isaiah, and Ezekiel), as well as the twelve minor prophets. The Ketuvim is a collection of twelve other books, including the *Psalms, Song of Songs*, and the *Book of Ruth*.

The Mishnah is the collection of all the disputes and commentary on Jewish law up to the 100s CE. It was compiled under the direction of Judah the Prince. Later, the Gemara was added to the Mishnah to make up the

Talmud. The Gemara is additional rabbinic teachings on every aspect of Jewish life. The material in the Talmud is divided into two categories: the **Aggadah**, which includes parables, sayings, sermons, and stories and is ethical, inspirational, or explanatory in nature, and the **Halakha**, commentary, discussions, and decisions related to Jewish law and practice.

Another work of note is the *Sefer Ha'Zohar*, commonly referred to as the *Zohar*. It is one of the books of the Kabbalah, the mystical aspect of Judaism, and focuses on such themes as angels, demons, charms, the coming of the Messiah, and numerology.

Holy Days

Shabbat, or the **Sabbath**, takes place from sundown on Friday night to sunset on Saturday. There are services Friday night and Saturday morning. Most Orthodox Jews are prohibited from engaging in work during this period.

Major holy days include:

- **Rosh Hashanah:** The Jewish New Year celebrated sometime between mid-September and early October
- **Yom Kippur:** The Day of Atonement, which includes fasting and contemplation; comes ten days after Rosh Hashanah
- **Sukkot:** Feast of Booths or Tabernacles, which celebrates the harvest and Yahweh's protection of the Jews during their forty years in the wilderness; nine days between late September and the end of October
- **Chanukah:** Festival of the Lights, also the Festival of Dedication, celebrating the victory of the Maccabees over the Greeks and Syrians in the 100s BCE and the rededication of the Temple in Jerusalem
- **Passover:** Celebrates the deliverance, or exodus, of the Hebrews out of Egypt; seders, special dinners, are held the first two and last two days; comes between March and April for eight days
- **Shavuot:** Celebrates the Yahweh's giving of the Ten Commandments to Moses; comes between late May and early June

The **menorah** is an important symbol of Chanukah. It holds nine candles, one for each of the eight nights of Chanukah and a ninth candle to light the others. According to the story of Chanukah, there was only enough oil for one night for the lamps in the Temple, but the oil lasted for eight nights. Each night of Chanukah, an additional candle is lit until all are lit the last night. The **Star of David**, probably the most recognized symbol of

Judaism today, is a six-pointed star created from two interwoven equilateral triangles. The star, or shield, as it is sometimes called, began to appear during the Middle Ages but was not solely representative of Judaism and appeared in many different places. Later, Kabbalists, or Jewish mystics, used the symbol to protect against evil. It became the official symbol of Judaism during the seventeenth century. Later, in Nazi Germany, Jews were required to wear a yellow Star of David as a method of identification.

Another symbol integral to Judaism is the **mezuzah**, a small piece of parchment paper containing the prayer Shema from the Bible. Encased in a small ceramic or metal case about three to five inches long, a mezuzah is mounted to the doorpost of the entry to the home and any room inside the home. Mezuzahs identify a home as Jewish and offer the inhabitants God's protection.

Hebrew school teaches Jewish children about their faith. It is typically held on Sundays and one weekday. For older students, it provides preparation for Bar Mitzvah for boys and Bat Mitzvah for girls, their coming-of-age ceremonies.

CHRISTIANITY

The focus of Christians is on the future: the redemptive power in their own lives of Jesus' resurrection. This message has resonated with millions of people since 33 CE, when Jesus was reported to have died for humankind's sins and then risen again. Today, there are over 2 billion Christians in the world belonging to three branches and more than a dozen denominations. Christianity is a continuation of the promise of the Old Testament but with a difference.

The History of Christianity

Jesus of Nazareth is a historical figure; he lived and died in the first century CE in Judea. He began preaching around the year 30 and quickly gained a following. His message was one of piety and the abandonment of sin and material things. In the Sermon on the Mount, he laid out a moral code, known as the **Beatitudes**, for his followers. He was seen as the Messiah promised by Yahweh, the Supreme Being, to the Jews, although they expected a kingdom on earth, whereas Jesus talked about a Day of Judgment when the good would be rewarded and the evil punished. (The word *messiah* translates as "christos" in Greek and Jesus became known as Jesus

Christ, that is, Jesus the Messiah.) He proclaimed himself the Son of God. When Jesus attacked the practices of some of the Jewish leaders, and as the crowds following him grew larger, the leaders determined to put a stop to his preaching. They convinced the Roman governor that his preaching was dangerous; the governor arrested Jesus and had him crucified like a common criminal.

After Jesus' death, resurrection, and ascension into heaven, his followers began to preach about Jesus and his mission, initially only among Jews. However, there were two schools of thought about the nature of Christianity: Was it a version of Judaism or a new religion? Some believed that it was a form of Judaism and should be presented only to Jews. Paul of Tarsus was a Jew but believed that it was a new religion that should be preached to everyone. Once a persecutor of Christians, he had converted in 35 CE after a vision and became a zealous missionary among gentiles.

The word of Jesus Christ and his teachings found receptive audiences wherever the new missionaries went, and, by the first century CE, they had attracted the attention of the government. At that time, the emperor was worshiped as a god. Christians mindful of the one God refused to obey and a period of persecution began, which continued more or less until the conversion of the Emperor Constantine to Christianity in 312. By the end of the fourth century, Christianity had become the official religion of the Roman Empire.

In the second century, Christianity had developed a formal organization of bishops and was centered in Rome. Peter had been the first bishop of Rome, and later popes would claim supremacy over the church as successors to Peter, citing Jesus' words: "Thou art Peter, and upon this rock I will build my church." The **Eucharist** as a celebration of the Lord's Supper had also developed as the central ritual. The title "Catholic," meaning "universal," came to identify the body of teachings of this church and included the Old Testament, the Gospels, and the Epistles of St. Paul.

In addition to adopting Christianity, Constantine established a new capital for the Roman Empire at the ancient site of Byzantium and named it Constantinople. Ultimately, his decision would lead to a schism in the Catholic Church in 1054 when the Western and Eastern branches split over doctrinal issues.

After the collapse of the Roman Empire in 476 and during the Middle Ages, the Catholic Church was often the most stable and unifying force in Western Europe as nomadic peoples moving out of Asia and Vikings from northern Europe invaded. By the sixteenth century, the hierarchy of the Roman Catholic Church in the West had amassed large fortunes, lived less than pious lives, and competed with temporal rulers for power. Into this mix, add disputes over doctrinal issues, and the time was ripe for the **Protestant Reformation**.

It should be noted that the Catholic Church answered the calls for reform generated by the Protestant Reformation with the **Council of Trent** that lasted from 1545 to 1563. Among the changes that the Council made were bishops had to live within their dioceses and preach regularly, seminaries to educate priests were to be erected in every diocese, and parish priests were to be better educated and actively minister to their parishioners. However, the Council reaffirmed a number of doctrines that were at the root of the Protestant reformation, namely:

- **The Role of Good Works in Salvation:** Grace, alone, as taught by several Protestant churches, was not enough for salvation
- **The Seven Sacraments:** Not all Protestant churches accept all seven sacraments
- **Transubstantiation:** The changing of bread and wine into the body and blood of Jesus during the act of consecration at Mass
- **Purgatory:** The place where the souls of sinners are purified after death and before entering heaven
- **Clerical Celibacy:** The belief that some or all members of the clergy are required to be unmarried
- **Veneration of the Saints, Relics, and Sacred Images:** Catholics honor and pray to them to intercede with God for them but do not worship these people and objects
- **Granting of Indulgences:** An indulgence is a remission of the temporal punishment that a priest has given a penitent to perform as a result of sinning. If not performed by the sinner, the sinner would suffer in purgatory. Beginning in the Middle Ages, sinners could give a small amount of money, considered alms, in exchange for an indulgence. By the time of the Reformation, indulgences had been extended to include those who had already died and were presumed to be suffering in purgatory. Indulgences had also become a lucrative way of raising money for the Church and Church leaders by preying on the fears of the faithful that they or their loved ones would languish in purgatory.

Major Christian Traditions

Christianity over the centuries has developed three main branches: the Roman Catholic Church, the Eastern Orthodox Church, and more than a dozen Protestant denominations.

....

TIP: It was the actions of a monk named John Tetzel, who was selling indulgences with the proceeds to be split by the Pope, who was interested in rebuilding St. Peter's Basilica in Rome, the local Archbishop in debt, and a bank, that drew Martin Luther's attention and precipitated the Protestant Reformation.

....

Roman Catholic Church

Until the **schism in 1054** between the Catholic Church in the West and the East, the history of Christianity was synonymous with the development of the Catholic Church. As noted above, the organizational structure of what became known as the Roman Catholic Church began as early as the first century CE with positions of priest and bishop. In time, the structure became increasingly hierarchical. The position of bishop of Rome was elevated to supremacy over all other bishops and was called "Pope." The position of cardinal, who oversaw a number of bishoprics, was added.

At various times and as early as the third century CE, the Church called councils of bishops and scholars to debate and affirm church doctrine. Among the results were such statements of dogma as the **Apostles Creed** and the **Nicene Creed**, which established certain precepts that Catholics had to accept. The Vatican Council of 1870 defined the doctrine of papal infallibility, though the concept had been in practice since the beginning of the Church. According to this principle, the Pope speaks infallibly when he proclaims a doctrine of faith and morals. Not all pronouncements of popes bear this weight. The most recent council was the Second Vatican Council held between 1962 and 1965, which sought to modernize Church practices and doctrines, including allowing Mass to be said in vernacular languages rather than Latin and eliminating the requirement that Catholics abstain from eating meat on Fridays.

Orthodox Church

Even before the schism, there were cultural and linguistic differences that evolved between Christian churches in the two parts of the former Roman Empire. The West spoke Latin and was influenced by Roman culture, whereas the Eastern part of the Empire had been deeply influenced by the Greeks and spoke Greek. Among the factors that caused the schism were the claim of the supremacy of the Pope of Rome in matters of faith and morals; the doctrine that raised the Holy Spirit equal to God the Father and God the Son; and an eighth-century controversy over the use of icons, highly ornate depictions of Jesus, Mary, and the saints.

There is no single Orthodox Church in that there are several national churches, for example, the Russian Orthodox Church and the Greek Orthodox Church. The Orthodox churches are overseen by a network of patriarchs, and there are a number of commonalities among them. There are also a number of doctrinal differences and practices that separate these Churches from the Roman Catholic Church:

- The Orthodox Churches do not recognize the primacy of the Pope.
- The Orthodox Churches do not accept the Holy Spirit to be on the same level as God the Father and God the Son, as Catholics do.
- Priests may marry in the Orthodox Churches before ordination, whereas the Roman Catholic Church forbids married priests.
- The Roman Catholic Church does not allow people to receive communion, that is, the Eucharist, before the age of seven, considered the age of reason. The Orthodox Churches allow infants to receive communion.
- The Roman Catholic Mass is said daily, whereas the Orthodox liturgy is not necessarily celebrated daily.
- The Roman Catholic Mass is only sung if it is specifically a High Mass. The Orthodox liturgy is always sung.
- Orthodox churches are highly decorated, especially with icons and gold decorations, whereas the typical Roman Catholic Church is less ornate.
- Orthodox churches accept the seven sacraments as the major sacraments, but believe that whatever the church does is sacramental.

Protestant Denominations

The basic elements that connect the various Protestant denominations are the importance of community and the power of the direct experience of God. In general, Protestants believe that salvation comes through God's gift of grace alone, accept the Bible as revealed and infallible truth, and do not require their priests or ministers to be celibate. Some faiths also accept female and gay clergy, unlike the Catholic Church. Statues and saints are not important and may not even be part of a denomination's theology. The emphasis is on preaching and singing, and services tend not to be daily.

There are two major doctrinal differences between Protestantism and Roman Catholicism: the Protestant belief in grace alone as the source for salvation and Jesus is present only symbolically in the Eucharist. Catholics believe that salvation comes from a combination of grace and good works and that Jesus, through the mystery of transubstantiation, is fully present in the Eucharist. (The Orthodox Churches also believe in transubstantiation and the combination of grace and good works as the path to salvation.)

The major Protestant denominations are:

- **Anglican/Church of England and Episcopalian:** Anglican is the original English church, and the Episcopalian church is the US counterpart. It split from the Roman Catholic Church when the Pope refused to allow King Henry VIII to divorce and remarry. Little changed in hierarchy or practice until the reign of Henry's third child, Elizabeth I. The Anglican Church is still closest in theological doctrine to the Roman Catholic Church.
- **Baptist:** Founded by Separatist John Smyth in Holland; spread to England and then to the American colonies during the First Great Awakening and later to the United States during the Second Great Awakening; agreed-upon theology and practices vary widely.
- **Congregational:** Founded on the ideas of Robert Browne; evolved from the Nonconformist movement in Great Britain that also fostered the Separatist or Puritan reform movement; important in Massachusetts Bay Colony.
- **Lutheran:** Founded by Martin Luther; doctrine of justification: belief that salvation comes through faith alone and the gift of grace; that is, good works are not counted.
- **Methodist:** Founded by John Wesley as a way to reform the Church of England; believes in the Trinity, accepts Baptism and the Eucharist as sacraments.
- **Presbyterian:** Founded on the ideas of John Calvin; emphasizes the doctrine of election: belief that God foreordained who would be saved (the elect) and who would not.
- **Seventh-Day Adventist:** Established in the United States in the mid-nineteenth century; observes Saturday as the Sabbath; believes that the Second Coming of Christ is near; accepts the Trinity and the Bible as infallible.
- **Unitarian:** Developed in the late eighteenth century and spread to the United States in the early nineteenth century; rejects the Trinity, original sin, predestination, and the infallibility of the Bible.

Christian Doctrine and Practice

Christians believe that Jesus was crucified for humankind's sins and rose from the dead on the third day. He remained with his disciples, teaching them for forty days, and then ascended into heaven. Jesus is seen as God made Man and, depending on the form of Christianity, as part of the Trinity of the Father, Son, and Holy Spirit. At Pentecost, fifty days after Easter (Christianity's most important holy day and the one that celebrates the resurrection of Jesus), the Holy Spirit came down upon the Apostles and they began to preach the message of Jesus.

Doctrines such as transubstantiation, the position of Mary, original sin, and infant baptism vary from religion to religion. For example, Catholics believe in original sin; it is the sin that Adam committed, and, because of it, all humans are born with this sin on their souls, but baptism removes it. For this reason, Catholics are baptized in infancy. (However, infants who die before they can be baptized are thought to be taken into heaven.) On the other hand, the Orthodox churches reject the concept of inherited guilt associated with original sin. The Orthodox churches also practice infant baptism, as do most Protestant churches. Some Protestant churches (e.g., branches of the Baptist denomination) generally practice adult baptism, believing that people are saved through God's gift of grace and baptism.

Sacred Writings

The Christian Bible is made up of the Hebrew Bible or Old Testament and the New Testament. The latter contains the Gospels of Matthew, Mark, Luke, and John and other writings, including the Acts of the Apostles, the Epistles, and the Book of Revelation, as well as thirteen pieces in the Hebrew Apocrypha. The Epistles are of special importance because they were written by Apostles and others to early Christian communities, discussing their issues and problems.

Depending on the branch or denomination of Christianity, the Bible is either considered to be the exact words of God or to have been inspired by God.

TIP: Some denominations support religious, or parochial, school systems, whereas others rely on religious instruction of the young during Sunday School sessions.

Holy Days

The major holy days of Christianity, depending on the branch or denomination, are:

- **Christmas:** Celebrates the birth of Jesus, or "God made Man"
- **Epiphany:** Celebrates the visit of the three Magi to the infant Jesus; twelve days after Christmas
- **Easter:** Celebrates Jesus' rising from the dead three days after being crucified by the Romans
- **Lent:** Forty days of fasting and prayer before Easter; begins on Ash Wednesday when Christians are reminded that "thou art dust and unto dust thou shalt return"
- **Palm Sunday:** Beginning of Holy Week; commemorates Jesus' entry into Jerusalem before his crucifixion
- **Holy Week:** Holy Thursday, which recognizes the Last Supper; Good Friday, which commemorates Jesus' death on the cross
- **Ascension Thursday:** Forty days after Easter Sunday; memorializes Jesus' ascent into heaven
- **Pentecost:** Sunday fifty days after Easter; celebrates the descent of the Holy Spirit on the Apostles and the beginning of the Christian church

In addition to these and depending on the branch of Christianity, there are other special days dedicated to the Virgin Mary and to various other saints. The dates for all of these holy days, as well as specific saints' days and when different parts of Scripture should be featured in religious ceremonies, are determined annually by the liturgical calendar.

ISLAM

Islam is the third monotheistic religion that developed in the Middle East. Muslims believe that Abraham, Jesus, and Muhammad are great prophets, and that Muhammad is the greatest and last prophet, the "Seal of the Prophets," who completes the revelations of God, the Supreme Being, or Allah, to humankind. The word *Islam* means "submission," and *Muslim* means "one who submits." In this case, Muslims submit to Allah.

The History of Islam

The historical founder is **Muhammad**, who lived from around 570 to 632 CE in what is today Saudi Arabia. However, Muslims believe that Muhammad was only a vehicle for Allah. Muhammad was born in Mecca, married, and became a wealthy merchant there. In 610 CE, at about age 40, he received the first of his revelations from Allah through the angel Gabriel. He began to preach the word of the one God, Allah, and to condemn the practice of idolatry among the city's inhabitants. As Muhammad began to gain followers, the authorities of Mecca became concerned and offered him bribes to stop. But Muhammad continued to preach his message of one God and religious piety. Finally, the authorities had had enough and began a campaign of persecution against Muhammad and his followers.

In 622, Muhammad fled Mecca and an assassination plot. His flight is called the Hegira. Muhammad found refuge in Medina, where he was able to bring together warring clans and become the leader of the city. Over the next ten years, his followers grew, and in 632, after years of fighting, they captured Mecca, founding the first Islamic state. Muhammad died shortly after.

After Muhammad's death, Islam continued to grow in numbers and in area, eventually becoming a vast political-religious empire that stretched across much of the Middle East, North Africa, and into Europe. The first four **caliphs**, as the leaders were known, are called the rightly guided, or orthodox, caliphs. They were relatives of Muhammad or had personally known him and were chosen by other Muslims to lead them. However, in 661, the Umayyad clan seized the caliphate from the fourth caliph, Ali, Muhammad's son-in-law, and shifted the focus of the caliphate to that of a temporal leader rather than a religious leader. The caliphate passed from dynasty to dynasty over the next centuries, and it was during these decades—from the eighth century through the thirteenth century—that Islam had what later came to be referred to as its Golden Age. Arabs and non-Arabs, Muslims and non-Muslims alike, all worked to translate major works of literature into Arabic, engaged in scientific discovery, and made advancements in math. Later, during the 1200s, the Ottoman state was formed by the Turks. It eventually grew into the Ottoman Empire and became a great Islamic empire and seat of Muslim power. The empire and the title of sultan, which had replaced caliph, ended after World War I.

In the early part of the 1500s, a Timurid king called Babur invaded the Indian Subcontinent and established the Mughal Empire. It was later ruled by his grandson, Akbar the Great, and encompassed what is today most of the Indian Subcontinent and Afghanistan. The Mughal Empire was unique in that, under Akbar, it encouraged "Goddism," a melding of Christian, Islamic, and Hindu religions. Later emperors discouraged this practice and instituted Shari'ah law.

Islam as a religion continued to grow. Today, more than a billion people worldwide consider themselves Muslims. Most belong to the Sunni branch, but Shi'a is the state religion of Iran. Other concentrations of Shi'ites can be found in India, Pakistan, and Iraq. Transcending all divisions is the **ummah**, the sense of community of believers. Madrasahs are Muslim educational institutions; they range from schools teaching young children to great universities. Their subjects range from the Qur'an to the Hadith to the law.

Major Islamic Traditions

Islam is divided into two branches: **Sunni** and **Shi'a**. The division goes back to the fourth caliph, Ali. Shi'ites believe that Ali should have been the first caliph and that his descendants are the rightful leaders of Islam, whereas the Sunnis believe that no leader was chosen by Muhammad to succeed him. To Sunnis, the four caliphs are the rightful heirs because they were chosen by Muslims themselves. Sunnis, who make up about 85 percent of Muslims, and Shi'ites also have doctrinal differences that divide them.

Sunnis do not have a religious hierarchy, but they do have **imams**, also called **mullahs**, who lead the community in prayer. Sunnis look for guidance in their lives to the Hadith; to Shari'ah, which is Islamic law; and to a consensus of interpretation between the Qur'an and Muslim scholars and leaders of the community. The Sunni form of Islam lends itself to interpretations, and no one set of interpretations is considered definitive. This flexibility has allowed it to embrace a number of cultures as it spread outward from its original location. Sunnis do believe in a **Madhi**, or Messiah, whose appearance on Earth will signal the beginning of an era of peace that will culminate in the end of the world.

Imams also lead Shi'ites in prayer. However, Shi'ites believe that their imams speak with special authority. They believe that the next Imam after Ali was Zain, Ali's son, who was followed by eleven more Imams. Known as Twelvers, they believe that the Twelfth Imam is still alive and still rules over them—though hidden from them—and that their imams are representatives of this Twelfth Imam.

A distinct part of both Sunni and Shi'ite branches of Islam is the **Sufi movement**, or the practice of mystical Islam. Sufis believe that the only way to have a relationship with God is through personal and direct experience. Though it is believed that Sufism began out of a practice of asceticism, this eventually became less of a main focus and only one of many tools to reach God. Sufis value kindness, patience, and love and use meditation and dancing to achieve a direct spiritual and mystical connection with God. Sufism developed into different orders, the most famous of which is the Mevlevi, whose founder Rumi is known worldwide for his mystical poetry.

Shi'ites believe that the Madhi will come one day and inaugurate a period of justice before the final end of the world. Shi'ites believe that the Qur'an must be interpreted rather than read literally, because it omits their belief that Muhammad designated Ali as his successor. For Shi'ites, religious and political authority rests not with community but with the imam. Ayatollahs are experts in Islamic law and religion; a Grand Ayatollah is an expert in religious studies and also a religious leader.

Wahhabism is a conservative movement that began on the Arabian Peninsula in 1744. Its founder Abd-al-Wahhab wanted to reform Islam and return it to what he considered the original, strict interpretation as found in the Qur'an. Wahhabism was adopted by the Sa'ud family that gained control of the kingdom in the early 1800s. Today, Wahhabism is the religion of Saudi Arabia and bound up with Saudi nationalism.

....

TIP: There is another Shi'ite sect called Seveners who believe that there were seven Imams.

....

Islamic Doctrine and Practice

According to the Qur'an, there are **Five Pillars**, or duties, that Muslims must perform and these are the foundational principles of Islam. Monotheism, the basic truth of Islam—that Allah is the one God—is revealed in the first pillar.

1. **Repeat the Shahadah, or Confession of Faith:** "There is no God but Allah and Muhammad is the Prophet of God."
2. **Perform Ritual Prayer:** Muslims are called to prayer five times a day and must face Mecca when praying. The five times are before sunrise, at noon, in mid-afternoon, at sunset, and at night before going to sleep.
3. **Fast:** Muslims must fast from sunrise to sunset during the month of Ramadan.
4. **Almsgiving:** Muslims contribute alms, known as **Zakat**, to the poor, typically 2.5 percent of their wealth.
5. **Pilgrimage (Hajj) to Mecca:** This must be done at least once during one's life. The central focus of Mecca is the Ka'bah, which Muslims must circle seven times and then touch or kiss the Black Stone that it houses. Muslims believe that the Black Stone was given to Adam by Allah and that Abraham and Ishmael, his son, built the Ka'bah to hold the Black Stone.

Muslims believe that each person must face Allah at the end of life and account for the way that he or she lived. While Muslims believe that life is submission, or surrender, to Allah, it is also a test. People have the ability to commit evil and will be held accountable for it. At the time of death, a person's body and soul are separated; on the day of judgment, Resurrection Day, souls and bodies will be reunited and judged by Allah. Those who lived good lives will go to paradise and those who lived evil lives will go to hell. Shari'ah is the term for the Islamic moral code and religious law that guides Muslims in their daily lives. Shari'ah law is derived from the Qur'an, the Haddith, and consensus of Islamic scholars. Together these lead to an understanding, or fiqh, of Islamic law.

Jihad is an important concept in the Muslim religion. *Jihad*, an Arab word that translates to "struggle," can be fought by Muslims in one of four distinct fashions: by the heart, the tongue, the hand, or the sword. The concept, considered a duty by all Muslims, is accomplished by fighting evil in one's heart, doing good through words (tongue) or deeds (hands), or physically fighting (sword) against those who are enemies of Islam and are considered nonbelievers.

Sacred Texts

The Qur'an is the major text of Islam; the word *Qur'an* means "reading" or "recitation." Muslims believe that the Qur'an is the exact words of Allah as revealed to Muhammad. There are 114 chapters, or **surahs**, arranged by length, not topic, and some 6,000 verses.

Hadith is a collection of traditions, analogies, and consensus. The traditions relate to the life and words of Muhammad and those of his companions, and the analogies and consensus are the result of the study of Muslim scholars endeavoring to answer questions, especially ones relating to legal issues and the duties of Muslims. There are thousands of hadith.

Holy Days

The holiest of Muslim celebrations is the month of **Ramadan**, which occurs in the ninth month of the Muslim calendar (the Muslim calendar has twelve months, but only 354 or 355 days). It honors the giving of the Qur'an to Muhammad. Muslims fast from sunrise to sunset each day for the month. **Id al-Fitr**, the Feast of Breaking the Fast of Ramadan, is celebrated at the end of the month.

Other holy days include:

- **Al-Hijrah:** The Muslim New Year; celebrates Muhammad's journey from Mecca to Medina
- **Mawlid al-Nabi:** Celebrates Muhammad's birthday
- **Laylat al-Qadr:** The Night of Power; occurs on the twenty-fifth day of Ramadan; honors the first revelation to Muhammad

RELIGIOUS MOVEMENTS AND SYNCRETISM

A religious movement may be defined as "a movement intended to bring about religious reforms." Using that definition, Buddhism and the Sunni branch of Islam can both be considered religious movements, as can any of the Protestant denominations. A number of such movements developed both before and after the beginning of the second millennium. In an attempt to reform religion, people tried to connect different aspects of various religions in ways they felt best served knowing god. This practice, called **religious syncretism**, can be seen in several of the movements that borrowed aspects of some religions but left behind others in their quest for spirituality.

Before 1000 CE

Mystery Cults

During the time of the Ancient Greeks, all citizens participated in state religious worship, though it did not meet the spiritual needs of some. Those individuals turned to what were known as mystery cults, or private groups open only to those who were initiated. These groups honored a particular god or goddess, oftentimes less popular or well-known gods. Popular figureheads of mystery cults included Dionysus and Demeter and even gods from other cultures, such as Egypt's Isis.

In order to participate in these secret cults, members had to endure a secret initiation. Once initiated, members gathered to dance, drink wine, and, often, have sex. The mystery cult that honored Dionysus, the Greek goddess of fruitfulness and wine, incorporated sexual relations among its activities. The mystery cult of Eleusis, named for the city where important agricultural festivals happened, also incorporated sexual relations into its cult activities during reenactments of the story of Hades and Kore.

At first mystery cults were exclusive and offered citizens a different experience than state religion. Some cults eventually lost their exclusivity, and anyone could decide to participate. Some even lost their religious character and become more like social clubs.

Jainism

Jainism began in the sixth century BCE in India as a reaction to some of the practices of Hinduism. Its traditional founder is **Mahavira**, who believed that he had found a way to stop the endless cycle of birth, life, and death. Like Hinduism, a person's karma determines his or her future lives, so Jains believe that only a person's own actions can end this cycle. Unlike Hindus, Jains believe that deities are of no help, so there is no reason to pray to them. Individuals must find release from the cycle of reincarnations through their own actions, and those actions should use as little effort as possible. Jainism is an ascetic religion. Those who are able to give up their material lives and become monks are closer to ending their cycle than those who remain "in the world."

The basic tenet of Jainism is that all living things have souls. As a result, Jains practice nonviolence. They also vow to speak truthfully and never take anything that they are not given. Jain monks also vow to be celibate and to renounce all attachments. Jains believe that attachment to material things keeps humans tied to the earthly life.

Zoroastrianism

Zoroastrianism is still practiced in parts of Iran and India, where adherents are known as **Parsis**. The religion began sometime between 1600 BCE and 1400 BCE, when the creator of goodness and life, **Ahura-Mazda**, revealed his truths to the prophet Zarathustra, also called Zoroaster. These truths are collected in the Zend-Avesta.

Zoroastrians believe that good and evil are fighting a battle for control of the universe and humanity. One force is Ahura-Mazda—representing good—and the other is **Ahriman**—the creator of evil and darkness. The battle will end in the final judgment, when the good will receive heaven and immortality and the evil will receive eternal punishment. To fulfill the will of Ahura-Mazda, Zoroastrians follow the threefold path: good thoughts, good words, and good deeds. Their liturgy consists of reciting from the Zend-Avesta and pilgrimages to holy fire-temples.

After 1000 CE

A number of religious movements have occurred in an attempt to bring about change. Lutheranism and other Protestant denominations, the Catholic Counter-Reformation, and Wahhabism all fit the definition of religious movements and were discussed earlier in the chapter.

Fundamentalism

A major movement that transcends religious boundaries is fundamentalism. Fundamentalists wish to return to the basic, or fundamental, tenets of their religion. In general, Christian fundamentalists believe that the Bible is the literal word of God and oppose many trends in modern society, such as abortion, same-sex marriage, and legal protections for women and homosexuals. On the other hand, along with some evangelical Christians, some fundamentalists push for increased environmentalism because they see humans as stewards of God's creation.

Islamic fundamentalists, known as Islamists, wish to strip all modernity from Islamic practices and reinstate theocratic government. The Taliban is an example of an Islamic fundamentalist group.

The Lubavitch, a missionary movement of the Hasidim, is a fundamentalist group within Judaism.

Sikhs

Sikhism began in the 1400s in Punjab, India, as a reaction to Hindu and Muslim practices that involved rituals, priests, and temples. A young Indian religious teacher, or **guru**, named Nanak felt that individuals needn't be a member of a particular caste or need the aid of a priest to have access to God. He believed that actions, more than words or rituals, brought one closer to God. He was the first of ten gurus that Sikhs later turned to for spiritual guidance.

Central to their beliefs is the understanding that there is only one God, with no physical form, and who resides in each individual. Sikhs believe that serving community and living a good, honest life, more so than devotion to the practice of religion, will help people to truly know God.

Baha'i

Baha'i, another movement that valued action over ritual or ceremony, originated in Iran in the mid-1800s. Baha'is believe that Moses, Abraham, Buddha, Muhammed, and Zoroaster were all prophets leading up to the arrival of Bahá'u'lláh, who brought a message of peace and justice. Bahá'is believe in the existence of a soul and the importance of prayer, meditation, and pilgrimages as ways to reinforce the connection between the soul and god. Like the message of Sikhism, Bahá'u'lláh's message stresses the importance of service to others as well behaving in noble and virtuous ways.

Contemporary Religious Movements

Evangelical Christians

Evangelical Christianity may seem like a modern phenomenon, but it began in Great Britain and from there was brought to the American colonies. It became the basis of the First Great Awakening, which took place from around 1720 until around 1760, and the Second Great Awakening of the 1790s through much of the nineteenth century. Evangelicals stress the need for personal conversion, known as being born again, and, like fundamentalists, place their trust in the authority of the Bible. They also emphasize the saving grace of Jesus' death and resurrection. Evangelical preachers of the Great Awakenings appealed to emotions and found a receptive audience among people for whom the erudite, emotionless sermons of the educated clergy held little appeal and few answers to the dangers and fears of the people. Modern evangelicals fill a similar need for contemporary people beset with fears and concerns about a world moving quickly and in ways that they may not understand or want.

Mormons

The **Church of Jesus Christ of Latter Day Saints**, known as the Mormon Church, is another Christian religious movement. Members believe that founder **Joseph Smith** was instructed by the angel Moroni where to find golden tablets containing the Book of Mormon, the history and teachings of the Nephite prophets. The Nephites were descended from one of the tribes of Israel that were scattered after the destruction of their kingdom. They traveled to the North American continent, and Moroni was the last prophet. The Mormons have an active mission to convert others to the original, true Christianity.

Ecumenism

The ecumenical movement was an effort of the Roman Catholic, Eastern Orthodox, and some Protestant churches to heal some of the divisions among them. Little progress was actually made, and the ordination of women and the inclusion of gays in the ministry have widened and hardened some divisions and have created new ones within some denominations, for example, the Anglican and Episcopalian churches.

Jehovah's Witnesses

Jehovah's Witnesses, or Bible Students as they were originally called, are members of a religious movement whose modern-day organization began at the end of the nineteenth century. The movement draws from Christianity but differs in its understanding of the Bible and its beliefs about the Holy Trinity, or God, Jesus Christ, and the Holy Spirit. Jehovah's Witnesses believe that God, or Jehovah, is the only true God. Jesus is the son of Jehovah but not equal to him, and the Trinity is a construct that resulted from pagan influences. In addition to these distinct differences, Jehovah's Witnesses believe that God wrote the Bible through the pens of others and believe it is a historically accurate account of God's word.

Jehovah's Witnesses believe that holidays such as Easter and Christmas have their roots in paganism, and so don't celebrate these or other holidays. They encourage followers to keep their lives simple to allow them as much time as possible for the most important aspect of their faith, **witnessing**. Witnessing involves walking door to door; sharing their beliefs; distributing copies of Bible-based literature, including the journals *The Watchtower* and *Awake*; and offering home Bible studies. Successful witnessing leads to repeat visits with the ultimate goal of converting individuals to their beliefs.

Jehovah's Witnesses do not believe in hell as a place of eternal torment; they believe that when a person dies, they simply stop existing. However, they do believe in an End Times, and point to passages in the Bible that indicate its coming. They believe that God's Kingdom is the solution to mankind's problems, and, as part of that kingdom arrangement, 144,000 people who are anointed by God will be resurrected to life in heaven to rule with Jesus in God's Kingdom. Those who do not go to heaven will remain in a paradise on Earth.

Scientology

The Church of Scientology was founded in the United States in 1954 by science fiction writer **L. Ron Hubbard**, following the success of his book *Dianetics: The Modern Science of Mental Health*. While his book dealt with the science of the mind, Scientology, the religion that evolved out of the success of this work, deals with the science of the spirit. Scientologists call this spirit the **thetan**; they believe that the thetan, or a person's true essence, has lived for thousands of years, inhabiting many different human bodies. Because man is a spiritual being, his unwanted emotions and negative thoughts (engrams) interfere with his attempt to reach the highest level of spirituality as a thetan. Specially trained auditors assist Scientologists in releasing engrams and achieving a "clear" state. This process goes on for eight levels, until the thetan reaches the level of All, or Infinity.

Though it doesn't have a sacred text similar to the Bible or the Qur'an, the religion is based on L. Ron Hubbard's extensive writings. Many courses and trainings exist to help practitioners continue to achieve a clear state, and strict adherence to these trainings is of utmost importance. Dedicated Scientologists are asked to sign a billion-year covenant showing that they will continue to spread the word about the religion in each new body their spirit inhabits.

Nature Spirituality

In addition to these movements, Earth-centered spirituality, or nature spirituality, is another movement that can be traced back to early mythology of many cultures and is still popular today. Earth-centered spirituality honors all of nature, offers little judgment, has no temples, and typically holds the view that the life force is female. Forces of nature and natural objects are celebrated, and practitioners thank the Earth goddess for the gifts of nature she has bestowed upon them. Earth-centered spirituality can be seen today as part of the Unitarian Universalist religious tradition.

SUMMING IT UP

- Shared dimensions of world religions include the **ritual, mythical, doctrinal, ethical, social,** and **experiential**. Approaches to the study of religion can be classified as **anthropological, phenomenological, psychological,** and **sociological**.

- **Indigenous religions** have certain characteristics in common: animism, magic, divination, totem, ancestor veneration or worship, sacrifice, taboos, myth, ritual, and rites of passage.

- **Native American religions** share certain characteristics. Generally, they are **animistic** and **polytheistic**; include a Supreme Being who created Earth and withdrew from it; have ceremonies, rituals, and taboos; do not practice human or animal sacrifice; include rites of passage, such as the vision quest; and have no special "priesthood" or hierarchy.

- **African religions** typically are **polytheistic**; have a central High God who created the world and withdrew from it; practice animism, ancestor veneration, and divination; make offerings and sacrifices of food; have rites of passage; and some have male and female priests and temples.

- An important aspect of **Egyptian religion** was the **cult of Isis and Osiris**, which spread across the Middle East and into Greece and the Roman Empire.

- In **Shintoism**, the divine resides in all things in nature; the word *Shinto* means "the way of the kami," meaning the spirits of the natural world. There exist three types of Shinto religion: **Shrine Shinto, Folk Shinto,** and **Sect Shinto**.

- **Hinduism** is polytheistic; the major deities are the **Triad: Brahma, Vishnu,** and **Shiva**. Hindus believe in Brahman, the Ultimate Reality; samsara; karma; moksha; and the four stages of life on the way to moksha.

- Four theistic paths exist in **Hinduism: Vaishnavism, Shaivism, Shaktism,** and **Smartism**. These paths honor a different god or group of gods and adhere to a particular path of enlightenment, or yoga practice.

- **Buddhism's** historical founder is **Siddhartha Gautama**. **Theravada Buddhism** and **Mahayana Buddhism** are its major sects; **Zen Buddhism** is popular in Japan, and Vajrayana, or **Tibetan Buddhism**, is very important in Tibet. Buddhism centers on the **Four Noble Truths** and the **Eight-Fold Path**.

- **Confucianism is a philosophy, not a religion.** Confucius taught that five relationships exist that involve reciprocal duties and responsibilities, or right action. The correct behavior, or conduct, is known as **li**.

- The traditional founder of **Daoism** is considered to be **Lao-zi**, also credited with writing the Dao De Jing, the basis of Daoism. *Dao* means "the way," and it is infinite and unceasing. It gives life and their nature to all things.

- **Jews** believe that **Yahweh** made a covenant to protect them in exchange for their worship. They believe that Yahweh gave Moses the Ten Commandments, the basic law, on Mount Sinai.
- **Jesus**, worshiped as the Son of God the Father, is the historical founder of **Christianity**. The Old and New Testaments are the central sacred writings of Christianity.
- **Muslims** believe that **Muhammad**, the historical founder of Islam, is the greatest and last prophet who completes the revelations of God, or **Allah**, to humankind. Islam has two branches: Sunni and Shi'a. The sacred writings of Islam are the Qur'an and the Hadith.
- The **Zoroastrian** creator of goodness and life, **Ahura-Mazda**, revealed his truths to the prophet **Zarathustra**, also called **Zoroaster**. These truths are collected in the Zend-vesta.
- **Greek Mystery Cults** offered citizens mysterious religious practices that differed from state religious worship, required initiation, and involved secret dances and rituals.
- A number of religious movements have arisen over the centuries, drawing from existing religious doctrine, in an attempt to reform existing religions or as reactions to the dogma and rituals of existing religions. Some of these movements include **Sikhism** and **Baha'i**, as well as **Mormonism, Scientology**, and **Jehovah's Witnesses**.
- **Earth-centered spirituality, or nature spirituality**, is another movement that can be traced back to early mythology of many cultures; its central figures are typically female, and worship is conducted in natural settings.

Chapter 4

Introduction to World Religions Post-Test

POST-TEST ANSWER SHEET

1. Ⓐ Ⓑ Ⓒ Ⓓ
2. Ⓐ Ⓑ Ⓒ Ⓓ
3. Ⓐ Ⓑ Ⓒ Ⓓ
4. Ⓐ Ⓑ Ⓒ Ⓓ
5. Ⓐ Ⓑ Ⓒ Ⓓ
6. Ⓐ Ⓑ Ⓒ Ⓓ
7. Ⓐ Ⓑ Ⓒ Ⓓ
8. Ⓐ Ⓑ Ⓒ Ⓓ
9. Ⓐ Ⓑ Ⓒ Ⓓ
10. Ⓐ Ⓑ Ⓒ Ⓓ
11. Ⓐ Ⓑ Ⓒ Ⓓ
12. Ⓐ Ⓑ Ⓒ Ⓓ
13. Ⓐ Ⓑ Ⓒ Ⓓ
14. Ⓐ Ⓑ Ⓒ Ⓓ
15. Ⓐ Ⓑ Ⓒ Ⓓ
16. Ⓐ Ⓑ Ⓒ Ⓓ

17. Ⓐ Ⓑ Ⓒ Ⓓ
18. Ⓐ Ⓑ Ⓒ Ⓓ
19. Ⓐ Ⓑ Ⓒ Ⓓ
20. Ⓐ Ⓑ Ⓒ Ⓓ
21. Ⓐ Ⓑ Ⓒ Ⓓ
22. Ⓐ Ⓑ Ⓒ Ⓓ
23. Ⓐ Ⓑ Ⓒ Ⓓ
24. Ⓐ Ⓑ Ⓒ Ⓓ
25. Ⓐ Ⓑ Ⓒ Ⓓ
26. Ⓐ Ⓑ Ⓒ Ⓓ
27. Ⓐ Ⓑ Ⓒ Ⓓ
28. Ⓐ Ⓑ Ⓒ Ⓓ
29. Ⓐ Ⓑ Ⓒ Ⓓ
30. Ⓐ Ⓑ Ⓒ Ⓓ
31. Ⓐ Ⓑ Ⓒ Ⓓ
32. Ⓐ Ⓑ Ⓒ Ⓓ

33. Ⓐ Ⓑ Ⓒ Ⓓ
34. Ⓐ Ⓑ Ⓒ Ⓓ
35. Ⓐ Ⓑ Ⓒ Ⓓ
36. Ⓐ Ⓑ Ⓒ Ⓓ
37. Ⓐ Ⓑ Ⓒ Ⓓ
38. Ⓐ Ⓑ Ⓒ Ⓓ
39. Ⓐ Ⓑ Ⓒ Ⓓ
40. Ⓐ Ⓑ Ⓒ Ⓓ
41. Ⓐ Ⓑ Ⓒ Ⓓ
42. Ⓐ Ⓑ Ⓒ Ⓓ
43. Ⓐ Ⓑ Ⓒ Ⓓ
44. Ⓐ Ⓑ Ⓒ Ⓓ
45. Ⓐ Ⓑ Ⓒ Ⓓ
46. Ⓐ Ⓑ Ⓒ Ⓓ
47. Ⓐ Ⓑ Ⓒ Ⓓ
48. Ⓐ Ⓑ Ⓒ Ⓓ

49. Ⓐ Ⓑ Ⓒ Ⓓ   **53.** Ⓐ Ⓑ Ⓒ Ⓓ   **57.** Ⓐ Ⓑ Ⓒ Ⓓ

50. Ⓐ Ⓑ Ⓒ Ⓓ   **54.** Ⓐ Ⓑ Ⓒ Ⓓ   **58.** Ⓐ Ⓑ Ⓒ Ⓓ

51. Ⓐ Ⓑ Ⓒ Ⓓ   **55.** Ⓐ Ⓑ Ⓒ Ⓓ   **59.** Ⓐ Ⓑ Ⓒ Ⓓ

52. Ⓐ Ⓑ Ⓒ Ⓓ   **56.** Ⓐ Ⓑ Ⓒ Ⓓ   **60.** Ⓐ Ⓑ Ⓒ Ⓓ

INTRODUCTION TO WORLD RELIGIONS POST-TEST

72 minutes — 60 questions

Directions: Carefully read each of the following 60 questions. Choose the best answer to each question and fill in the corresponding circle on the answer sheet. The Answer Key and Explanations can be found following this post-test.

1. Which religion celebrates Diwali, the Festival of Lights?

   A. Judaism
   B. Islam
   C. Mahayana Buddhism
   D. Hinduism

2. According to Shinto, which of the following are earthly and heavenly spirits?

   A. Kami
   B. Koan
   C. Karma
   D. Li

3. Paul is important in the history of Christianity because he

   A. wrote one of the four Gospels.
   B. was the first bishop of Rome.
   C. believed that Christianity was more than a Jewish sect.
   D. converted the Emperor Constantine to Christianity.

4. The break between the Roman Catholic Church and the Eastern Church in 1054 is called a

   A. heresy.
   B. schism.
   C. sect.
   D. denomination.

5. Which of the following best describes the Dao?

   A. Fundamental presence in all things
   B. Harmony with nature
   C. Self-awareness
   D. Simplicity

6. Two epic poems are of great importance to the Hindu religion:
   the *Mahabharata*, which describes two Indian families who are
   fighting for control of a kingdom in a bloody war, and one that
   describes the wanderings of Prince Rama and his wife Sita. The
   latter is known as the

   A. *Bhagavad Gita.*
   B. *Ramayana.*
   C. *Tripitaka.*
   D. Hadith

7. Eating pork is considered taboo in

   A. Islam.
   B. Hinduism.
   C. Buddhism.
   D. Shinto.

8. The Hindu theistic tradition or path that worships all five deities
   (Vishnu, Shiva, Shakti, Ganesh, and Surya) is called

   A. Vaishnavism.
   B. Smartism.
   C. Shaktism.
   D. Shaivism.

9. Which of the following might a Buddhist do to improve his or her
   karma?

   A. Remove shoes before entering a mosque to pray
   B. Rinse one's mouth and wash one's hands before entering a
      shrine to pray
   C. Offer a bowl of food to a monk
   D. Pray to one's ancestors

10. Which of the following is/are reciprocal relationships described by Confucius?

>   I. Father and son
>   II. Brother and sister
>   III. Ruler and subject

   A. I only
   B. I and II only
   C. II and III only
   D. I and III only

11. The angel Moroni appeared to

   A. Moses.
   B. Joseph Smith.
   C. Muhammad.
   D. Abraham.

12. A network of patriarchs is the form of organization in

   A. Lutheranism.
   B. Judaism.
   C. Eastern Orthodox churches.
   D. the Anglican Church.

13. Jains believe that

   A. a life devoted to monasticism is not helpful or necessary in finding release from reincarnation.
   B. praying to the deities will aid humans in their quest for release from reincarnation.
   C. release from the cycle of reincarnation comes through one's own actions.
   D. celibacy is unnatural.

14. Why are Catholics baptized?

   A. As a reminder of Jesus' death and resurrection
   B. To affirm that they are born again in Christ
   C. To remove the stain of original sin
   D. To make amends for the sin of Adam

15. What is the cause of suffering according to Daoism?

    A. Unnaturalness

    B. Violence

    C. Desire

    D. The innate evil in the world

16. Which of the following best describes a bodhisattva in Mahayana Buddhism?

    A. A yogi master

    B. A Buddhist monk

    C. Anyone working toward enlightenment

    D. Someone who has achieved nirvana, but remains in life to help others to enlightenment

17. The Aztec practiced human sacrifice to

    A. ensure a good harvest.

    B. prevent the end of the world.

    C. thank the deities for victory in battle.

    D. instill fear in their enemies.

18. Which of the following describes a way that an anthropologist would study a religion?

    A. Compare taboos across three religions

    B. Question subjects on what a worship service means to them

    C. Observe an initiation rite for an adolescent

    D. Investigate the impact of a church's outreach to the homeless

19. Dharma is the

    A. cycle of birth, death, and rebirth in Buddhism.

    B. release from the cycle of reincarnation in Hinduism.

    C. religious and moral duties of individuals in Hinduism.

    D. name given to Buddhas-in-waiting.

20. Which of the following sacraments removes original sin?

    A. Confirmation

    B. Baptism

    C. Eucharist

    D. Penance, also called Confession

21. At a madrasah, a person would

    A. study the Talmud.
    B. make an offering to the kami.
    C. make an offering to Vishnu.
    D. study the Qur'an.

22. God as the Creator or Supreme Being is a concept found in

    I. Christianity.
    II. Judaism.
    III. Northern Native American religions.
    IV. Islam.

    A. I and II only
    B. I and IV only
    C. I, II, and IV only
    D. I, II, III, and IV

23. In which of the following would you find icons?

    A. Russian Orthodox church
    B. Roman Catholic church
    C. Mosque
    D. Buddhist temple

24. What insight about life, death, and rebirth did Gautama receive that "enlightened" him about how to live one's life?

    A. Monasticism is the proper way to receive enlightenment.
    B. Life must be lived on a middle path between asceticism and desire.
    C. Practicing yoga and meditation are the only way to enlightenment.
    D. All reality is one with Brahman.

25. All of the following are steps in the Eight-Fold Path EXCEPT:

    A. Right understanding
    B. Right speech
    C. Right action
    D. Right loyalty

26. Which of the following statements best describes Islamists?

    A. They preside over religious courts.
    B. Their goal is to reestablish theocratic states.
    C. They are scholars of Islamic law.
    D. They lead the faithful in prayer services at mosques.

27. Which of the following men urged Jews to leave their ghettoes and live within their larger communities in the nineteenth century?

    A. Maimonides
    B. Mordecai Kaplan
    C. Moses Mendelssohn
    D. Baal Shem Tov

28. Islam existed as a vast political-religious empire that stretched across much of the Middle East, North Africa, and into Europe, but ended after

    A. World War I.
    B. World War II.
    C. 661 CE.
    D. the 1500s.

29. The influence of Martin Luther on later Protestant denominations can be seen in their adoption of his doctrine of

    A. salvation through faith alone.
    B. baptism as the only sacrament.
    C. the continuation of the central role of priests/ministers in confession.
    D. the continuation of Latin for services.

30. What is the Hindu name for the ultimate reality?

    A. Yin and yang
    B. Ahimsa
    C. Brahman
    D. Atman

31. The Ka'bah is sacred to Muslims because

    A. they believe that Abraham and Ishmael built it.
    B. it is where the angel Gabriel appeared to Muhammad.
    C. it houses Muhammad's grave.
    D. it is where Muhammad ascended into heaven.

32. Which of the following believed that human nature is evil?

    A. Confucius
    B. Mencius Meng-Zi
    C. Hsun Tzu Xun-Zi
    D. Lao-zi

33. The Talmud contains the

    I. Mishnah.
    II. Gemara.
    III. Haggadah.
    IV. Torah.

    A. I and II only
    B. I and III only
    C. I, II, and III only
    D. I, II, III, and IV

34. Typically, religions have ceremonies honoring which of the following rites of passage?

    I. Death
    II. Birth
    III. Marriage
    IV. Puberty

    A. I and II only
    B. I, II, and III only
    C. I, II, and IV only
    D. I, II, III, and IV

35. The Bavenda, or Venda, religious tradition of Africa honors a supreme being referred to as

    A. Zwidutwane.
    B. Raluvhimba.
    C. Awa.
    D. Binu.

36. According to Buddhism, what is the cause of suffering?

    A. Desire
    B. Striving after a good reputation
    C. Material goods
    D. Human attachments

37. Social virtue, or *jen*, is a basic concept of

    A. Islam.
    B. Shintoism.
    C. Buddhism.
    D. Confucianism.

38. Kosher laws relate to

    A. whom Jews may marry.
    B. what Jews may and may not do on the Sabbath.
    C. what Jews may wear.
    D. what Jews may and may not eat.

39. The division between Sunni and Shi'ite Muslims has its origins in

    A. the dispute over who was the rightful heir of Muhammad.
    B. how strictly to interpret the Qur'an.
    C. what the proper role of women is in Islam.
    D. disagreements over the position of imams in Islam.

40. Jainism developed over dissatisfaction with aspects of

    A. Buddhism.
    B. Hinduism.
    C. Shinto.
    D. Confucianism.

41. Rosh Hashanah celebrates the

    A. victory of the Maccabees and the rededication of the Temple in Jerusalem.
    B. harvest.
    C. Jewish New Year.
    D. exodus from Egypt.

42. Which of the following is a reason for the schism between the Roman Catholic and Eastern Orthodox churches in 1054?

    A. The Eastern Orthodox Church practices adult baptism, and the Roman Catholic Church practices infant baptism.
    B. The Eastern Orthodox Church does not allow any kind of ornamentation, whereas the Roman Catholic Church does.
    C. The Roman Catholic Church claims that the Pope has supremacy over all other churches in matters of faith and morals.
    D. The Orthodox Church accepts married clergy, as long as they were married before ordination.

43. Ummah is the

    A. niche in the wall of a mosque or a design in a prayer rug pointed in the direction of Mecca during prayer.
    B. call to prayer five times a day.
    C. pilgrimage to Mecca.
    D. community of the faithful.

44. The major divisions of Islam are

    A. Sufi and Shari'ah.
    B. Sunni and Wahhabism.
    C. Shi'a and Sunni.
    D. Twelvers and Shi'a

45. Buddhism differs from Islam in that Buddhism

    A. does not have a historical founder, but Islam does.
    B. practices polytheism, but Islam is monotheistic.
    C. calls its God Buddha and Islam calls its God Allah.
    D. does not have the concept of a single supreme being, but Islam does.

46. All of the following are offshoots of Islam EXCEPT:

    A. Sikhism
    B. Jainism
    C. Wahhabism
    D. Sufism

47. In 622 CE, Muhammad fled Mecca because of an assassination plot; his flight is called the

A. Umayyad.
B. Hadith.
C. Medina.
D. Hegira.

48. Which of the following is a tenet of Confucianism but NOT Daoism?

A. Right action
B. God as creator
C. Harmony
D. The less government, the better

49. The Hindu caste system is documented in which of the following?

A. *Law of Manu*
B. *Rigveda*
C. *Ramayana*
D. Varna

50. Which of the following best describes the outcome of the Council of Trent?

A. It ignored issues raised by the Reformation.
B. It reaffirmed Catholic doctrine.
C. It made significant changes to Catholic doctrine in a conciliatory gesture that was not reciprocated.
D. It was an attempt to modernize the Catholic Church.

51. Which of the following honors the first revelation to Muhammad by the angel Gabriel?

A. Id al-Fitr
B. Al-Hijrah
C. Laylat al-Qadr
D. Ramadan

52. Which of the following groups observes the Sabbath most strictly?

    A. Orthodox Jews
    B. Reform Jews
    C. Conservative Jews
    D. Reconstructionist Jews

53. All of the following developed as ways to preserve Judaism through early centuries of persecution EXCEPT:

    A. Synagogues as the center of worship
    B. The development of mystical elements in Jewish teaching
    C. The rabbi as teacher and explicator
    D. Designating Saturday as the Sabbath based on the Book of Genesis

54. Daoism was seen as a complement to, rather than a rival of,

    A. Hinduism.
    B. Shintoism.
    C. Theravada Buddhism.
    D. Confucianism.

55. The basic belief system of Buddhism is/are the

    A. Mishnah.
    B. Four Noble Truths.
    C. Five Pillars.
    D. Analects.

56. In indigenous religions, which religious personage foretells the future?

    A. Animist
    B. Healer
    C. Diviner
    D. Medicine man and woman

57. The triad of Hindu deities is

    A. Brahma, Krishna, and Shakti.
    B. Brahma, Vishnu, and Shiva.
    C. Shiva, Shakti, and Krishna.
    D. Vishnu, Rama, and Kali.

58. In order to know God, Sikhs believe that an individual must

    A. be of the correct caste.
    B. adhere to a specific meditation practice.
    C. worship in a certain temple.
    D. live a good, honest life.

59. The name of which of the following religions means "submission"?

    A. Catholic
    B. Islam
    C. Orthodox
    D. Buddhism

60. Hinduism draws from the beliefs of the Aryans, who worshiped deities that represented beauty and the forces of nature. These deities included

    A. Abraham and Moses.
    B. Matthew, Mark, Luke, and John.
    C. Indra, Agni, Varna, and Soma.
    D. Apsu and Tiamat.

ANSWER KEY AND EXPLANATIONS

1. D	13. C	25. D	37. D	49. A
2. A	14. C	26. B	38. D	50. B
3. C	15. A	27. C	39. A	51. C
4. B	16. D	28. A	40. B	52. A
5. A	17. B	29. A	41. C	53. B
6. B	18. C	30. C	42. C	54. D
7. A	19. C	31. A	43. D	55. B
8. B	20. B	32. C	44. C	56. C
9. C	21. D	33. A	45. D	57. B
10. D	22. D	34. D	46. B	58. D
11. B	23. A	35. B	47. D	59. B
12. C	24. B	36. A	48. A	60. C

1. **The correct answer is D.** Hindus celebrate Diwali, the Festival of Lights, in autumn. The celebration includes a thorough house-cleaning to welcome Laksmi, the female deity of wealth. You might be confused by the term "Festival of Lights" because it's also an English translation for the Jewish celebration, Chanukah, but *Diwali* is the operative word.

2. **The correct answer is A.** In Shintoism, Kami are the spirits or essences of the natural world. Koan (choice B) are used in Zen Buddhism to help people reach enlightenment. The law of karma (choice C) is the determinant in the kind of future lives a person will have, according to Hinduism and Buddhism. Li (choice D) is the principle of correct behavior between individuals in Confucianism..

3. **The correct answer is C.** Paul is important because he believed that Christianity was a completely new religion. Choice A is incorrect because the Gospels were written by Matthew, Mark, Luke, and John. Peter is believed to have been the first bishop of Rome, so choice B is incorrect. Choice D is incorrect because Paul lived in the first century CE, and Constantine was converted after a vision in 312 CE.

4. **The correct answer is B.** A schism is a split between entities caused by differences in opinion or belief. Doctrinal issues caused the schism in 1054. A heresy (choice A) is a belief in conflict with the orthodox, that is, official, teachings of a church. A sect (choice C) is a small group that has broken from an established church; the qualifier "small" doesn't fit the size of either the Roman Catholic or Eastern Churches. A denomination (choice D) is a type of religious body and is larger than a sect.

5. **The correct answer is A.** The Dao is the fundamental presence or essence in all things. The question asks for a description of the Dao, not a definition of the word. Choices B and D are incorrect, although Daoists seek harmony with nature and simplicity in their lives. Achieving self-awareness (choice C) is not an explicit goal of Daoism.

6. **The correct answer is B.** The *Ramayana* is the second poem of great importance to the Hindu religion. The *Bhagavad Gita* (choice A) is a poem found within the *Mahabharata*. The *Tripitaka* (choice C) is one of the sacred writings of Theravada Buddhism. The Hadith (choice D) is one of the sacred writings of Islam.

7. **The correct answer is A.** Islam prohibits Muslims from eating pork; it is taboo in their religion. Judaism, which also originated in the Middle East, also prohibits the consumption of pork. Choice B is incorrect because pork is not taboo for Hindus, but eating beef is. Choices C and D are incorrect because pork is not taboo for either Buddhists or Shintoists.

8. **The correct answer is B.** Smartists worship all five deities with the same level of reverence. Vaishnavism (choice A) is the theistic path that worships Vishnu. Shaktism (choice C) is the theistic path that worships Shakti. Shaivism (choice D) is the theistic path that worships Shiva.

9. **The correct answer is C.** Actions to improve one's karma, such as providing food to monks, are known as making merit. Choice A is incorrect because the word *mosque* signals that the shoe removal before entering is a practice of Muslims, not Buddhists. Choice B is incorrect because washing before entering a shrine to pray is a ritual of Shinto. Choice D is incorrect because Buddhists do not venerate their ancestors.

10. **The correct answer is D.** The reciprocal relationships taught by Confucius include that of father and son (I) and ruler and subject (III). Choice A is incorrect because it omits the ruler and subject relationship. Confucius doesn't mention sisters, so choices B and C cannot be correct.

11. **The correct answer is B.** Moroni appeared to Joseph Smith, gave him the golden tablets that are the sacred writings of the Church of Jesus Christ of Latter Day Saints, and gave him the ability to translate them into English. Choice A is incorrect because Yahweh appeared to Moses in the form of a burning bush on Mount Sinai. Choice C is incorrect because the angel Gabriel appeared to Muhammad. Choice D is incorrect because Yahweh appeared to Abraham.

12. **The correct answer is C.** The Orthodox churches are overseen by a network of patriarchs. Lutheran churches are organized into synods overseen by ministers, so choice A is incorrect. Judaism (choice B) has no organized structure of overseers. The highest clerical office in the Anglican Church, or Church of England (choice D), is the Archbishop of Canterbury.

13. **The correct answer is C.** Jains believe that release from the cycle of reincarnation comes only through one's own actions. Choice A is incorrect because Jains believe that monks are closer to release than those who live in the world. Choice B is the opposite of what Jains believe, which is prayer is of no help in attaining release. Choice D is incorrect because Jain monks take vows of celibacy.

14. **The correct answer is C.** Catholics believe that all humans are born with Adam's sin on their souls and that baptism removes it. Choice A may seem like a good answer, but it's not the reason why Catholics are baptized. Choice B hints at being a "born again" Christian (someone who believes in adult baptism), but Catholics believe in infant baptism, so this choice is incorrect. Choice D is incorrect because baptism removes the sin inherited from Adam, but doesn't make amends for it.

15. **The correct answer is A.** According to Daoism, unnaturalness is the cause of suffering, pain, and violence. Violence (choice B) is but one result of unnaturalness. Choice C is incorrect because Buddhists believe that desire is the cause of suffering. Choice D is incorrect because the Daoists don't consider evil as a cause for suffering; evil in the world would be another result of unnaturalness.

16. **The correct answer is D.** In Mahayana Buddhism, a bodhisattva may also be someone who has achieved nirvana, died, and is now prayed to by other Buddhists. Choice A is incorrect because yoga in its various forms is found in Hinduism, not Buddhism. Choice B is incorrect because a Buddhist monk is not yet a bodhisattva. Choice C is incorrect because a bodhisattva has already achieved nirvana.

17. **The correct answer is B.** The Aztec believed that by offering human sacrifices to the gods, they could prevent the end of the world. Choices A, C, and D are plausible but incorrect.

18. **The correct answer is C.** An anthropologist would observe an adolescent initiation rite. Choice A describes how a follower of the phenomenologist school of thought would study religion. Choice B is incorrect because a psychologist would study how religion influences thoughts and behavior. Choice D is an approach that a sociologist might take.

19. **The correct answer is C.** Dharma is the religious and moral duties of individuals in Hinduism. The cycle of reincarnation described in choice A is called samsara in both Hinduism and Buddhism. Choice B is incorrect because moksha is the release from the cycle of reincarnation. Choice D is incorrect because Buddhas-in-waiting are called bodhisattvas.

20. **The correct answer is B.** According to the Catholic Church, baptism removes original sin. Confirmation (choice A) is the sacrament that initiates the believer into full and mature participation in the Church. Choice C is incorrect because the sacrament of the Eucharist is the body and blood of Jesus. Choice D is incorrect because the sacrament of Penance removes the sins that individuals themselves commit.

21. **The correct answer is D.** A madrasah is an Islamic school, so students would study the Qur'an. Choice A is incorrect because a student would study the Jewish Talmud at a yeshiva. Choice B is incorrect because a person would make an offering to a kami at a Shinto shrine; the names of the shrines vary depending on whom the shrine honors. Choice C is incorrect because a Hindu would make an offering to Vishnu at a mender, a Hindu temple.

22. **The correct answer is D.** A supreme being or creator of all things—whether known as God, Yahweh, the High God, or Allah—is a concept found in Christianity, Judaism, Native North American religions, and Islam. Only choice D has all four answers.

23. **The correct answer is A.** Icons, highly ornate depictions of Jesus, Mary, and saints, decorate Eastern Orthodox churches, so you find icons in Russian Orthodox churches. Roman Catholic churches (choice B) are less ornate. Mosques (choice C) and Buddhist temples (choice D) are places of worship for non-Christian religions. Choice C is also incorrect for another reason: Muslims believe that representations of Muhammad are blasphemous.

24. **The correct answer is B.** Buddha's enlightenment about a middle path led to the Eight-Fold Path and the Four Noble Truths. Monasticism (choice A) is a practice found in Theravada Buddhism, and the belief that yoga and meditation are the only way to enlightenment (choice C) is taught in Zen Buddhism, but neither was what prompted the Buddha's enlightenment. Worship of Brahma (choice D) is a tenet of Hinduism.

25. **The correct answer is D.** Right understanding (choice A), right speech (choice B), and right action (choice C) are all aspects, of the Eight-Fold Path of Buddhism. Right loyalty, which is not one of the aspects, is the correct answer.

26. **The correct answer is B.** Islamists are Muslim fundamentalists who want to return Islam to what they consider its original teachings. Choice A is incorrect because religious courts are typically presided over by clerics. Choice C is incorrect because those who study Islamic law are called mujtahid. Imams lead the faithful in prayer at mosques, so choice D is incorrect.

27. **The correct answer is C.** Moses Mendelssohn encouraged Jews to move out of the ghetto and into the modern European world. Jewish scholar Maimonides (choice A) lived in the late twelfth and early thirteenth centuries. Mordecai Kaplan (choice B) is credited as a founding thinker of Reconstructionist Judaism, which originated in the United States in the 1920s and 1930s. Baal Shem Tov (choice D) preached that Jews should maintain their identity and live apart from the secular world.

28. **The correct answer is A.** The Golden Age of Islam ended after World War I, not World War II (choice B). Choice C is incorrect because the Umayyad clan seized the caliphate from the fourth caliph, Ali, Muhammad's son-in-law, in 661, but this didn't end the power of the empire. Choice D is incorrect because it was during the 1500s that the Ottoman Turks seized control of the empire. Though they changed the title of the empire's leader from caliph to sultan, the empire continued.

29. **The correct answer is A.** Even if you weren't sure about the other answers, Luther's concept of justification by faith should have stood out as the correct answer. It was a monumental change in Christian theology. Choice B is incorrect because Luther accepted baptism and the Eucharist as sacraments. Choice C is incorrect because Luther didn't accept the rite of confession to a priest. Choice D is incorrect because Luther introduced the use of the vernacular, in his case, German, for services and for scripture.

30. **The correct answer is C.** Hindus believe that Brahman is the ultimate reality. Yin and yang (choice A) are concepts in Daoism that represent balance. Ahimsa (choice B) is the Hindu and Buddhist principle of nonviolence. Atman (choice D) is the self or soul to Hindus.

31. **The correct answer is A.** Muslims believe that Abraham and Ishmael built the Ka'bah as a resting place for the Black Stone given to Adam by Allah. Choice B is incorrect because Gabriel appeared to Muhammad in various places but not in the Ka'bah. Choice C is incorrect because Muhammad ascended into heaven, so there is no grave. Choice D is incorrect because the site of the ascension was the Dome of the Rock in Jerusalem.

32. **The correct answer is C.** Hsun Tzu Xun-Zi was a later Confucian scholar who believed that human nature was inherently evil, in contrast to Mencius Meng-Zi (choice B), who believed that human nature was inherently good. Confucius (choice A) believed in the natural goodness of people. Lao-zi (choice D) is the traditional founder of Daoism.

33. **The correct answer is A.** The Talmud contains the Mishnah, a collection of disputes and commentary on Jewish law up to the 100s CE, and the Gemara, additional rabbinic teachings on Jewish life. The Haggadah is the service for a Seder and the Torah is the first five books of the Hebrew Bible. Choices B and C are incorrect because they contain the Haggadah. Choice D is incorrect because it contains both the Haggadah and the Torah.

34. **The correct answer is D.** In general, world religions have ritual ceremonies to celebrate or mark death, birth, marriage, and puberty. Only choice D includes all four, so it is the correct answer.

35. **The correct answer is B.** Raluvhimba is the supreme being worshiped by the Bavenda or Venda. Zwidutwane (choice A) is the name that Bavenda call the water spirits. Awa (choice C) is what the Dogon refer to as their cult of the dead. Binu (choice D) is the Dogon name for special places, or shrines, where they honor their ancestors.

36. **The correct answer is A.** The best answer is always the most complete, and while striving after a good reputation (choice B), material goods (choice C), and human attachments (choice D) are all things that can cause suffering, they are specific causes. The best answer for this question is desire, which encompasses the other answers.

37. **The correct answer is D.** *Jen*, translated as social virtue and also as humaneness, is a basic concept of Confucianism. It is not a concept taught in Islam (choice A), Shintoism (choice B), or Buddhism (choice C).

38. **The correct answer is D.** Kosher laws are dietary laws describing what foods and combinations of foods Jews may and may not eat. There are 620 mitzvah, or commandments, plus commentary in Jewish law that relate to marriage (choice A), activities on the Sabbath (choice B), and other elements of Jewish life such as dress and grooming (choice C), but they are not kosher laws.

39. **The correct answer is A.** Interpretation of the Qur'an (choice B), the role of women in Islam (choice C), and the positions of imams (choice D) may be differences that have developed between Sunni and Shi'a Muslims, but the dispute over who was the rightful heir of Muhammad is the origin of any differences that have developed over the centuries.

40. **The correct answer is B.** Both Jainism and Buddhism developed because of dissatisfaction with aspects of Hinduism. Choice A is incorrect because Buddhism itself developed as a reaction to elements of Hinduism. Choices C and D are incorrect because Jainism is not related to either Shintoism or Confucianism.

41. **The correct answer is C.** Rosh Hashanah celebrates the Jewish New Year. The celebration of the victory of the Maccabees and the rededication of the Temple in Jerusalem (choice A) is Chanukah, known as the Festival of Lights or the Feast of the Dedication. Sukkot, the Feast of the Tabernacle, celebrates the harvest (choice B). Passover celebrates the exodus from Egypt (choice D).

42. **The correct answer is C.** In contrast to the Roman Catholic Church, the Orthodox Churches do not recognize the primacy of the Pope. Choice A is incorrect because both churches practice infant baptism. Choice B is a misstatement of the controversy over icons that was one of the reasons that precipitated the schism. The emperor in the East in the early 700s came under the influence of Islam and ordered churches to remove their religious imagery. The Pope condemned this iconoclasm, destruction of icons, or representations, as heresy. In time, the Eastern Church returned to the use of icons as symbols. Choice D is a difference between the Roman Catholic and Eastern Orthodox Churches but not a reason that brought about the schism, so it's incorrect.

43. **The correct answer is D.** The ummah is the community of faithful Muslims, which transcends all branch divisions. The wall niche or rug design pointed in the direction of Mecca (choice A) is called the mihrab. The call to prayer (choice B) is the adman. Hajj (choice C) is the pilgrimage to Mecca.

44. **The correct answer is C.** Islam divided into Shi'a and Sunni in a dispute over who was the legitimate successor to Muhammad. Choice A is incorrect because Sufism is a mystical branch of Islam but is not a major division; Shari'ah is Islamic law, not a religious division. Choice B is incorrect because Wahhabism is a conservative movement within Islam that originated on the Arabian Peninsula. It is not a major division of Islam. Choice D is incorrect because Twelvers are another name given to Shi'ites who believe that there have been Twelve Imams and the Twelfth and last is still alive and hidden to them.

45. **The correct answer is D.** There is no ultimate being in Buddhism. Choice A is incorrect because both Buddhism and Islam have historical founders, Gautama Buddha and Muhammad, respectively. Choice B is incorrect because Buddhism is not polytheistic; however, Islam is monotheistic, worshiping only Allah. Choice C is incorrect because, although the God of Islam is Allah, Buddha is not the same as a supreme being.

46. **The correct answer is B.** Jainism was founded as a reaction against Hinduism. Sikhism (choice A) was founded by Guru Nanak in the late 1400s and early 1500s as a reaction to both Islam and Hinduism. It preaches monotheism and includes the concepts of karma, dharma, and reincarnation. Wahhabism (choice C) is a very conservative form of Islam that developed in Saudi Arabia. Sufism (choice D) is the mystical tradition within Islam.

47. **The correct answer is D.** Muhammad's flight from Mecca is called the Hegira. The Umayyad (choice A) was a clan that seized the caliphate from the fourth caliph, Ali, Muhammad's son-in-law. The Hadith (choice B) is a collection of traditions, analogies, and consensus that relate to the life and words of Muhammad and his companions, as well as the study of Muslim scholars relating to legal issues and the duties of Muslims. Medina (choice C) is the name of the second holiest city in Islam and the place where Muhammad found refuge when he fled Mecca.

48. **The correct answer is A.** Confucianism believes in the need for right action, whereas Daoists believe in the need for inaction. Choice B is incorrect because neither Confucianism nor Daoism includes a supreme being who created the world. Choice C is incorrect because harmony is a basic principle of Daoism, not Confucianism. Choice D is incorrect because the Daoists believe that the less the government governed, the better. On the other hand, Confucianism teaches that it is the duty of the government to provide for the well-being of the governed.

49. **The correct answer is A.** The Hindi caste system is described in the *Law of Manu. Rigveda* (choice B) is a collection of more than a thousand hymns. The *Ramayana* (choice C) is an epic poem about Prince Rama and his wife. Varna (choice D) is the name of the caste system.

50. **The correct answer is B.** The Council of Trent made changes to certain abuses of Church practices but reaffirmed all issues of dogma. Choice A is incorrect because the Council of Trent was convened because of the Reformation and took up issues highlighted by the Reformation. Choice C is incorrect because the Council made no changes to doctrine. Choice D describes the Second Vatican Council.

51. **The correct answer is C.** Laylat al-Qadr honors the first revelation to Muhammad by the angel Gabriel. Id al-Fitr (choice A) is known as the Breaking of the Fast of Ramadan. Al-Hijrah (choice B) celebrates Muhammad's journey to Medina from Mecca. Ramadan (choice D) is the month of fasting.

52. **The correct answer is A.** Orthodox Jews are the strictest in their observance of Jewish traditions and religious doctrines and practices.

53. **The correct answer is B.** Choice B refers to the Kabbalah, a body of mystical teachings that was collected in several volumes and doesn't relate to efforts of the ancient Jews to preserve their identity through centuries of persecution. Using synagogues as the centers of worship (choice A), appointing rabbis as teachers and explicators (choice C), and designating Saturday as the Sabbath based on the Book of Genesis (choice D) are traditions that Jews followed to preserve their identity and religion.

54. **The correct answer is D.** Daoism was seen as a complement to the rigid etiquette of Confucianism and flourished in China for several centuries. However, as Theravada Buddhism (choice C) spread in China, a rivalry developed between adherents of the two religions. Over the centuries, rulers influenced by one or the other of the religions persecuted its rival adherents. However, over time, Daoism and Theravada Buddhism, along with Confucianism, became firmly established as major religions among the Chinese. Neither Hinduism (choice A) nor Shintoism (choice B) became forces within Chinese religious life.

55. **The correct answer is B.** Buddhism centers on the Four Noble Truths and the Eight-Fold Path. The Mishnah (choice A) is the collection of all the disputes and commentary on Jewish law up to the second century CE. It is one part of the Talmud. The Five Pillars (choice C) are the basic belief system of Islam. The Analects (choice D) collect the teachings of Confucius.

56. **The correct answer is C.** The diviner has the power to see into the future; among the ancient Greeks, the person able to do this was called an oracle. Choice A is incorrect because an animist believes that the objects of the natural world, such as rocks, are spiritually alive, but an animist doesn't foretell future events. *Healer* (choice B) and *medicine man/woman* (choice D) are different terms for people who cure the sick.

57. **The correct answer is B.** The three major deities, or triad, of Hinduism are Brahma, Vishnu, and Shiva. Choice A is incorrect because although Krishna is an incarnation of Vishnu, it's not the same. Shakti is the wife of Shiva but not one of the triad. Choice C is incorrect in part because it contains Shakti and also because Krishna is an incarnation of Vishnu, but not the same. Choice D is incorrect because Rama is an incarnation of Vishnu, and Kali is another name for Shakti, the wife of Shiva.

58. **The correct answer is D.** Being of the correct caste (choice A), adhering to a specific meditation practice (choice B), and worshiping in a certain temple (choice C) are all things that other religions, such as Hinduism and Buddhism, ask of followers in order to know God. Sikhs feel that one can know God without those things, as long as one lives an honest and good life.

59. **The correct answer is B.** The word *Islam* means "submission," and *Muslim* means "one who submits." *Catholic* (choice A) means "universal." *Orthodox* (choice C) means "conforming to established beliefs." *Buddhism* (choice D) is derived from a Sanskrit word meaning "the enlightened one."

60. **The correct answer is C.** The Aryans worshiped the deities Indra, Agni, Varna, and Soma. Abraham and Moses (choice A) were historical figures in Islam and Judaism. Matthew, Mark, Luke, and John (choice B)were authors of the Gospels found in the New Testament. Apsu and Tiamat (chocie D) are names of the main Mesopotamian gods.